THE M   T

How A.

Of These Extraordinary Women

FEW International Publications

Quantity order requests can be emailed to:
Kimberly@thefewwomen.com

The Miracle Effect
Publishing Coordinator: Kimberly Joy Krueger

Contributing Authors: Heather Taylor, Marlene Mackey Dawson, Paula H. Mayer, Tracy Hennes, Tara Johnson-Brower, Rebecca Grambort, Janet Byrne, Luanne Nelson, Kimberly Joy Krueger, Sue Sherstad, Maureen Hurd, Candice Moe Julie Nowak, Cindy Christofferson, Mary Kay Swittel, Tamara Fink, Mary Markham, Wendy Leppert, Denise Coop

Contributing Editors: Reji Laberje, Bucket List to Bookshelf, and Marla McKenna

Cover Design: Nada Orlic, Nada Orlic Design
Interior Layout: Reji Laberje, Bucket List To Bookshelf

Photos and Graphics Courtesy of: Kimberly Laberge, Reji Laberje, Nada Orlic, Justin Taylor, Lara Landon, Tara Johnson-Brower, Rebecca Grambort, Janet Byrne, Luanne Nelson, Kimberly Joy Krueger, Sue Sherstad, Maureen Hurd, Candice Moe, and Denise Coop.

Marketing and Publicity Footage: Kimberly Laberge

Publicity: Kimberly Joy Krueger, Reji Laberje, Contributing Authors

ISBN-10 1979140995
SBN-13: 978-1979140997

Categories:
Religion & Spirituality/Christian Books & Bibles/Literature & Fiction/Collections & Anthologies
Religion & Spirituality/Christian Books & Bibles/Biographies
Biographies & Memoirs/Reference & Collections

FEW INTERNATIONAL PUBLICATIONS
An Extraordinary Publishing Experience

FEW International Publications is for women authors at all levels who are seeking more from telling their stories than just a printed project. FEW Authors, publishing under four unique lines of books, want to learn and grow through the experience of creating a written work that impacts others and glorifies God.

Extraordinary Women; Extraordinary Stories

http://kimberlyjoykrueger.com/few.php

TABLE OF CONTENTS

Albert Einstein:

"There are only two ways to live your life. One is as though nothing is a miracle. The other is as though everything is a miracle."

HEATHER
TAYLOR

Heather Taylor started her writing career at the young age of sixteen when she entered a poetry contest and earned a spot in their Poetry Anthology Series. Along with writing, she also co-Hosts a radio show, makes speaking appearances, and writes a blog called All I Know is... Heather's relatable personality and compassionate heart make it easy to understand why she enjoys speaking to women and teenagers in need. Through sharing her struggles with depression and other bumps in the road, Heather uses her "in your face" sense of humor to help people find hope. Contact and Follow Heather at: HJTenterprise@gmail.com and at: alliknowis.wordpress.com.

— Chapter 1 —

THE TWENTY YEAR MIRACLE

Heather Taylor

"Do not be misled: 'Bad company corrupts good character.'"

👈*1 Corinthians 15:33 (NIV)*

I once thought my never-ending story was one of hopelessness. I had reached a point in my life where I wanted to scream, truly scream from the depths of my pain all the way out to the top of my voice asking God, begging him, to change something, maybe even everything about my life? Well, I didn't just want to scream...I did. Were you ever desperate enough to put down your pride and any other false idols you had been worshipping to pick up the hand of God and allow Him to lift you out of the valley?

I've been in a place that many have gone, but far too few have been able to escape. I've seen darkness overcome the light and watched silently in my mind as I destroyed everything God had given to me. Just as I was contemplating ending my pain by ending my life, God began to work miracle after miracle to fix my broken world, mend my broken heart and fill my life with a new kind of love that I had never known. This is my Miracle story.

From the outside, I had what looked like a really good life but, on the inside, I was battling a very large, very dark demon named depression.

Nobody in my life knew about my struggle at the time, not even me. I didn't know there was a name for it. I just thought I was moody and sad a lot. I spent the majority of my time putting on an overly fake smile and trying to be the life of the party so nobody would see me for who I really was: a sad, overweight, miserable woman who had just about given up on life. I wouldn't say I was ready to commit suicide yet, but I had definitely become hopeless.

I had definitely become hopeless.

I married my first and only true love at nineteen. He was twenty-one. People warned us we were too young, but we both knew it was right. We loved each other so much back then and I'm happy to say we still do to this day. With that being said, there was something we didn't know then that really would have come in handy. We didn't know how to communicate to each other. We couldn't listen to each other or express a complaint without getting our feelings hurt badly. So badly, in fact, that we allowed a tremendous distance to come between us. We started to become different people and we started to go our separate ways.

Terry, my husband, and I had not only been fighting more but we had also started letting outside influences into our home and that led me to feeling more depressed, confused, and guilty. We were and still are Christians, but during this time what normally would have been a strict "NO" like drinking too much, making bad financial choices, or allowing people in our lives that did things we didn't approve of; often became a soft *"Maybe"* and many times turned into a whispered or unspoken *"yes"*.

I had also made a new friend around the time that Terry and I were having troubles and, as my friendship with her grew, I began to put her first in my life...and my husband a weak second. So, eventually, he befriended her as well. She turned out to be a long lasting bad habit that God continuously tried to remove from my life. I considered her to be my best friend and overlooked a lot of red flags because she helped both me and my husband, to "have fun".

We allowed this woman into the inner circle of our marriage, both dependent on her, as a distraction from working on one another. She went on family vacations with us, without her husband. There was no separation. She often relied on my husband to do husbandly duties for her, like fix something, hang something up, or other "traditionally male" tasks. Her friendship with him was close, but I overlooked it because she was fun-loving. It all started innocently enough. (After all, Satan doesn't pop in all of a sudden, rather bit by bit.)

Eventually, Terry and I would go on dates...plus her, sometimes even adjusting our schedules and plans to ensure that it

COULD include her. I'm embarrassed to say that we sometimes even let her stay overnight in our home...in our bedroom. And the fact that there wasn't sex happening didn't make it any less of a marriage of three. The boundaries were blurred. I allowed this poisonous friendship to influence my growing frustration with Terry and manipulate me into thinking he was untrustworthy and selfish. I wasn't who I should have been around her or, more importantly, who I wanted to be.

Meanwhile, I was also battling another demon but this one was internal. I started to truly hate myself and the things I was thinking and doing. My mind would constantly remind me of every negative I had ever said or done. I told myself over and over that I was a bad wife, a horrible house keeper (well that one actually is true); I was ugly, fat, and repulsive. I couldn't stand to look in the mirror and if someone complimented me for anything, I instantly assumed they were lying. The worst lie I allowed myself to believe was that I was a bad mother and that my children deserved better. This lie was probably the one that threw me over the edge.

> *I started to truly hate myself.*

I was drowning in my own pool of lies and self-pity fed to me by the enemy. I wanted the pain and guilt to be gone. *I* wanted to be gone. I was a wife, a mom to two small children, Brooke and Lyndsey, a full time home maker and, in my mind, a complete failure at *all* of those things. I was filled with self-hatred, especially after gaining over a hundred pounds due to two surgeries, three pregnancies, a miscarriage, and then eating to fill the emptiness I felt. I knew I had to fix my life...or end it!

One afternoon, after having a long and very loud fight with my husband, Terry took the girls and went to his mother's house. What's ridiculous is, at this point in our relationship, we went from being each other's everything to being more like roommates...adults who just happened to share space. Every time we spoke, we fought. It was probably over something small because—by then—everything small became big.

I started to sob as I walked into my laundry room to start a load of laundry. It was something I seldom was able to drag myself to do, anymore. There were piles and piles of laundry all over the floor. You could tell they had been separated by colors, lights, darks, and whites, but never quite made it to the final process of being placed into the washer. When you get into a hole of depression, even the simplest task seems extremely overwhelming. You have to climb out of the pit just to get to level ground, in order to do a dish, take a shower, sweep a floor. Everything takes effort and energy. You get so overwhelmed that you decide you're better off getting back into bed. Having a shower once a week was good for me. I'm not sure how I was still able to take care of my kids. I remember the process of separating the laundry and how it had been so exhausting that, afterward, I had to just walk away. By this time, the piles had been there for so long that the air in the laundry room was thick and stale. It smelled like dirty socks and old towels.

When I looked around the room, it all hit me at once. The constant arguing - the chaos that seemed to become my normal everyday life now was too much. I could feel my head spin and knew, if I didn't sit, I was going to fall. I landed in the middle of three very large, very rancid-smelling piles. Each pile was larger than the other and each one's smell more potent than the one before. I felt like I might vomit, so I placed my hands on the side of my head to help steady the spinning and began taking shallow breaths through my mouth. I scanned the room for something, I don't know what, or maybe it wasn't a specific thing at all; maybe I thought–in the midst of the piles of dirty, unwashed clothes–I would find the answers to how my life got this out of control. Whatever the reason was, whatever I was hoping to find, I didn't find it and that made me feel completely defeated.

I felt my body start to shake and my lips start to quiver as I tried to take in a deep breath of the putrid air. I struggled to hold it in for a moment longer when my body simply defied me and released my breath along with a heart-wrenching, ear-piercing scream that felt like it came from the depths of my soul. Tears began racing down my face as I lost all control. I allowed the rest of my body to fall to the floor and I wrapped myself up into the fetal position right there in the middle of the mess. I can still remember the feeling of my knees squishing my chest, making it hard to breath because I had wrapped my arms around them so tightly in an effort to comfort myself by rocking.

This was it! I couldn't do this, anymore!

Just like the pile of clothes I was laying next to seemed like Mount Everest, my life seemed like an overwhelming climb that I couldn't survive. The mountains of laundry around me were just one of the many side effects of my reckless decisions and complete surrender to depression.

The stench that now filled my nostrils and caused my eyes to burn was like smelling salts.

It was my final wake up call.

I didn't want to be this person anymore!

I didn't want to be the person standing at the bottom of the mountain!

I wanted to attack my mountain!

I wanted to reach that summit, even if my mountain was a pile of moldy, unwashed clothes.

I wanted to conquer it!

I remember thinking once that people who let God into their life begin to go through trials and tribulations, but the truth is you cry out to God as a last resort when your life is *already* filled with trials and tribulations. He was my last resort. I remember it as if it were yesterday, screaming God's name and begging him to "fix this!" I knew I would not make it another day, hour, minute, or second without God saving me. I begged him through my sobbing, sniffling, shaky breaths to fix the mess I had made. I begged him to clean my mess and make me whole again. I cried out to my Lord and savior to save me. I asked him to come into my heart and help me learn to lean on him and love him like I had before. I asked him to forgive me for feeding my flesh and not my soul.

All I had to do was ask and I finally did.

God heard me that day I laid on my laundry room floor in the fetal position rocking myself and weeping. He heard my screams, my cries, and my tears. He wanted to save me; all I had to do was ask and I finally did.

I lay down in the laundry room for hours, gasping and crying, until I actually fell asleep, right there in the piles of filth. It was a complete breakdown. My miracle was put inside of me while I slept. It's as if God took me to the laundry room to cleanse me. While I slept, He took out my soul, rinsed it clean, gave it back, and...

. . . I woke up *clean.*

Things began to change after that day on the floor. *I* started to change. One of the main things I had asked God to "fix" in my life was the company that I kept. I wanted to get closer to God and I knew that wasn't going to happen while hanging around with the people we had surrounded ourselves with. God intervened for me and my family and literally moved us 1100 miles away from the situation we were in...the opportunity opened up just days after my prayer. I knew I still would have to do my part by truly guarding my heart and only keeping people in my life that helped me be a better person. I also knew that God was now in control and he could make anything possible. I call this time in our life "The Beginning of my Twenty Year Miracle".

We moved to Delafield, Wisconsin on November 1, 1997, because of a well-deserved but extremely unexpected job promotion.   We told our friends and family that it was his Employer's idea of a joke to offer a promotion with just one string attached…you had to live in the frozen tundra.

This promotion came just days after my laundry room prayer and needed to be filled fast. We put our house on the market in September and had it sold, packed up, and moved out heading to Wisconsin in two months. We sold our home by ourselves and managed to get $10,000.00 above appraisal. The first and only couple that looked at it bought it for asking price! God meant business and so did we. We were ready for a new life.

Wisconsin started off a little bumpy. For starters, we were all alone. There was nobody to rely on other than each other and that got a little weary after three months. I started to get upset and, if I'm being completely honest, I started to really resent my husband for taking me away from my family and friends. We began falling into the same pattern of throwing blame and making accusations to one another. I began to feel hopeless again.

My oldest daughter, Brooke, who was eight at the time, had asked a little girl from across the street, Taylor, to come over. They played for awhile and I sent her home with cookies. After Taylor left I was busying myself with clean-up and getting ready to make dinner when the phone began to ring. It may not have seemed like a big deal to most people, but our phone hadn't rung in three months, so it was a big deal to me. I picked it up, unsure of whom would be on the other end, and when I heard her voice I was even more confused.

A very friendly, very Wisconsin voice shot over from the other side of the receiver and proceeded to thank me for the "amazing" cookies that I had sent home with Taylor. "That was so sweet of you to think of us. Taylor said she had such a good time over there and that you guys are from Florida? This weather must be a shock for you guys!" said the very friendly woman on the phone.

"Yes, it takes some getting used to for sure." I was never very good at talking on the phone in general but talking to a stranger was close to number one on my HATE list.

"My kids are so happy to have other children to play with in the neighborhood. Taylor mentioned you guys are Christians, have you found a church home yet?"

My eyes shot up into my skull! Okay, here it was. Her daughter had asked me if I was a Christian earlier when she was about to leave. I felt really uncomfortable talking to her daughter about this, but talking to the Mom about this made uncomfortable feel like a tickle! For some strange reason, I allowed the conversation to continue. "Well, ummm, we really haven't been here that long so we haven't had time to check many churches out yet."

"Oh, well which ones have you been to?"

Okay now she caught me in a lie! "I'm really not sure of the names." I stuttered.

"Which denomination did you go to?" the curious Jesus Freak on the other side of the phone asked.

Oh My Lord what is up with this lady? I had to end this conversation. "Well, we are like non-denominational. We are just Christians!" I could hear her thinking on the other side of the phone.

She paused a minute and then said "But you do know the Lord, right? You believe that Jesus died for your sins?"

_____

But you do know the Lord, right?

_____

Enough was enough! "Of course, yes, of course I do!" I had never in my life experienced someone soooo pushy. I quickly decided that this woman was a Jesus Freak for sure and I wanted nothing to do with her. "Well listen, I want to thank you for calling and for also letting Brooke Play with Taylor. Maybe we can let THEM play together again sometime?" Why I thought she would take the hint is beyond me, but she definitely did not.

"Yes, I think Taylor would love that. I would love to invite you guys to visit our church this Sunday. If your whole family can't make it maybe Brooke could come with us?"

Like that was gonna happen I thought to myself! "Oh wow, thanks so much. I will have to think about that and get back to you. I better go now though because my husband is going to be here any minute and I am just starting dinner. Thanks again for the call." I quickly hung up the phone and swore to myself silently I would never talk to that woman again! God had other plans.

My relentless Jesus Freak neighbor was everything I was not. She spoke about God as if he were a "real" person in her life and not this mythical Character that I had been raised to know. She made him seem real and, before too long, I was hooked. I found myself calling *her* and inviting her (and her six children) over. I felt like a sponge around her that was completely wrung out and needed fluid. She would fill me with God's truth, light, and love. She shared the word of God with me like no other person ever had before. She showed me his love, his yearning for me to have my heart's desire.

She was a true gift from God and, despite that first call, it didn't take me long to figure it out. She WAS the answer to my prayer asking that God help me with the company I keep. I have always said that God has a wonderful sense of humor and this woman, my friend, Kim, in my life, was just one more thing to prove my point.

We were so different in every way, but we soon became fast friends. I think we bonded over our love of cooking and eating. She had a huge family and wanted more! I was very happy with my two girls and did not see another child anywhere in the future. Her love for the Lord showed in everything she did and I was just starting to get to know him. She and her husband lived a very modest life and while he worked she would home school their children! No way was I going to do that! Through all of the differences that we seemed to have, we got along famously. She and her family quickly became our Wisconsin family. We spent our days going from one house to the other. My daughters became best friends with her daughters and I ended up falling in love with all of her children including the five more she would go on to have. This woman, The Jesus Freak, was the answer to my prayer. I knew pretty quickly that she was my miracle. I know that may sound funny, but miracles can come in many ways. Some of them are gigantic and indubitable, but others are simplistic and quiet (not that I'd ever call my friend "quiet").

I know in my heart that God sent me 1100 miles away to save me and used this woman to help me learn about his love, and to teach me how to love, and to lean on him. During the time we lived in Wisconsin, which was almost exactly three years, I learned to trust God and believe his promises. I learned by example and my example was my Jesus Freak.

> *God sent me 1100 miles away to save me.*

Kimberly Krueger has continued to be my mentor and dear friend throughout the years. God used her to teach me and he continues to use her to help other women every day. I have told her before I may have been the first one she saved, but I am nowhere near the last! I truly believe that the message I am supposed to share is the miracle of friendship. I know it isn't big and in your face, but it changed my life.

God can move mountains but he can also quietly and beautifully use an unexpected friendship to save a life. God placed me in her life so she could help me through my brokenness. Just by being a shining example of God's love and living to glorify his name she lead me back to my Father. I was shown how to lean on him in my marriage, motherhood, and relationships. God delivered me from anger and bitterness and showed me how to forgive. She helped me learn how to trust him for everything.

Kim is still in my life and, although I only lived next door to her for a short time, she has been in my heart and my family's hearts, ever since. We have known each other for twenty years and, although she is still a Jesus fanatic with twelve children, I am so thankful that God sent me to live next door to her; she is my Twenty-Year Miracle and a single miracle that led to many others.

But *that*, as they say, is another story. Lucky for me, God's story never ends...

Joyce Meyer:

"Fear is a dead end, but faith always has a future."

MARLENE
MACKEY
DAWSON

Marlene Dawson is a retired Special Education paraprofessional. When she discovered that God loved her, and wanted her to help others, her desire for women to know about God and His love became deeply rooted in her heart. Marlene knows what courage it takes to face life's painful circumstances, and pursue healing. She is part of a ministry team that helps women move forward from difficult situations. Marlene is also a conference speaker who teaches on faith, healing, and prayer. Marlene enjoys grandparenting, traveling, and writing. She and her husband live in Wisconsin.

——— Chapter 2 ———

WHITE STONE FROM JESUS

Marlene Mackey Dawson

"My dear brothers and sisters, take note of this: Everyone should be quick to listen, slow to speak and slow to become angry, because human anger does not produce the righteousness that God desires."

🙖*James 1:19-20 (NIV)*

By the time I was five years old, I knew he would kill me if I ever told. I knew because he said he would. In all the years that followed, I complied with his demands. I protected him far more than I protected myself; children don't know these things. The abuse began when I was in diapers and continued until I was nearly

23

seventeen years old. There were more than four hundred situations, including: rapes and other physical abuses, as well as verbal and emotional abuse. Dad often said it was my fault he abused me. I don't know how he persuaded me, but I believed him. He was my dad; surely he would not lie to me. In the midst of pain and terror, I began to see God's presence manifest in my life, what I call kisses from heaven.

Dad was in the military until I was twelve. After he retired, we moved often. From birth through high school, I lived in fifteen cities in ten states, and on two continents. Moving was hard on mom and the family, but I was grateful. It was a built-in protector. I never got close enough to anyone to let my guard down. Keeping his secrets kept me safe. Mom knew of only one abuse incident, which occurred when we lived in England.

After World War II, Great Britain transformed some of its country estates into apartments for American families. We lived in Lush Hill Manor, on a mountaintop near Castle Eton. There was a ranch nearby, with children the same ages as my older brother and me. The four of us rode their mountain ponies in the hills often, kisses from heaven.

Our apartment was small, but livable for a family of seven. My sister and I shared bunk beds; I had the lower bunk. One night at about one thirty A.M., mom heard one of us moaning. Thinking someone was sick, she checked on us. I was the one moaning, but not because I was ill. Dad was on top of me on my bed. He had one hand on my mouth, and his other hand and mouth were in places they shouldn't have been. My jammies were mostly off. He was wearing boxers, and they were pulled down. I thought, *if she finds out what's going on, he will kill me.*

She left the room, and his assault became more invasive.

Mom came back quickly.

She began hitting him with a metal dustpan on his head and shoulders. She was yelling. I was crying. His hands were all over me.

Mom grabbed his hair and pulled him off me, and out of my bed. She yelled at him to go get dressed, and then she comforted me. I was eight years old.

Mom did everything right. She called the Commander and the Chaplain. The Military Police came and arrested dad, and the Chaplain was at our house within the hour. Mom decided to take us back to the States. In a few days, we were on a plane flying across the ocean after arriving in London only months before. It broke my heart to leave England.

One day at my grandparents' home in North Carolina, Mom said, "Not all men are like your father." It wasn't much, but it gave me hope. I had several months of safety and peaceful sleep there, more heavenly kisses. While dad's assaults and threats kept me quiet, God's kisses kept me stable.

Soon after dad came back from England, we transferred to Missouri. We lived on base, near the pool, my "home away from home." I was asked to teach kindergarten swim classes, giving me two more hours away from home. Swimming was a lifesaver, another kiss. I was on guard around dad, though.

I was in fifth grade. Two of my siblings were in second and third grades. This was when report cards had satisfactory or unsatisfactory marks for behavior and attitudes. I usually had straight A's and satisfactory marks. I learned to separate the abuse from the rest of my life. I rarely showed negative feelings. No one could suspect what I dealt with several nights a week. My younger siblings couldn't hide their anxiety. Between them, they had seventeen unsatisfactory marks on their report cards. Naturally, we were all scared about what dad would do.

"It's not your fault; it's your sister's fault. She's supposed to watch you," dad said menacingly.

He grabbed my wrist, and dragged me to their bedroom.

"No, Dad!" I begged.

"I told you to watch your brother and sister! This will teach you to obey me," he threatened.

He grabbed his belt with the shiny, hard buckle. He told me to pull my shorts down. He folded the belt and drew his hand back. I tightened every muscle in my ten year old body. When the belt struck, I flinched, but didn't cry. This made him angrier. WHAP! WHAP! The belt hit my little butt, still no sound from me. It hurt! Tears were pouring down my face. I'm pretty sure I was in shock. And the hits just kept coming.

Four...five...six... My mind kept count.

"Bud, stop it!" Mom screamed. He pushed me face down on the bed.

Seven...eight...nine... Counting was all I had left. Ten...eleven... A pause. Was he stopping? No. He opened the belt so the buckle end would make contact. Twelve...thirteen... The prong penetrated my skin! I finally screamed.

Seven...eight...nine... Counting was all I had left. Ten...eleven...

"Daddy, I'm sorry! I promise to watch the kids! PLEASE!" Fourteen...fifteen...

"BUD! STOP! SHE'S BLEEDING!" Mom pleaded and screamed even more.

He must have shoved her, as she fell less than three feet from me. There was no escape now. Sixteen…seventeen…

The hammering stopped. He threw the belt on the floor and stormed out.

I was hysterical. I thought I was going to die. I didn't think anything else.

I became aware of Mom holding something soft against my leg. The buckle hits were on the back and side of my left thigh. Once I was calmer, Mom got some first aid supplies, and cleaned and bandaged the wounds. I was in bed the next two days, and then I went back to school as if nothing happened.

When we got our next report cards, we were scared. I had my usual grades and marks. Although my brother and sister were doing better, they had eleven unsatisfactory marks between them. We waited anxiously. When dad finally got to our report cards, he looked at me, then turned to the younger ones and said, "Why can't you two be more like your sister Marlene? She always has perfect grades."

In the summer of 1967, realization dawned. My best friend was spending the night. I was wide awake, fearful that my dad would come in my room. I knew this was not normal. Whenever I slept at her house, there was no concern about her dad. I always thought it happened in every home, but nobody talked about it. Awareness filled me with shame. Believing it was my fault was deeply ingrained. It was terrifying to wake up, finding him assaulting me every way he could. It was even more important to keep the secrets. I wanted to live.

The next summer I had my driver's license, bought a car, and had two part-time jobs. Life was as normal as it could be. The tension between my parents began to escalate. This meant the abuse was also escalating. One evening in July, my folks went out dancing with friends. They got home after midnight, but I was up reading. Both were in a good mood, chatting about their evening. Dad was carrying a six pack of beer. He gave me a nod on his way to the bathroom. Mom walked to the closet to hang her jacket.

"Marlene, wait until you hear what happened!" Mom laughed.

As she turned from the closet, she regaled me with a story about a dancer. Dad rounded the corner and glanced in our direction, six pack still in hand. I was facing him, but mom was facing me. His face changed from a smile to rage. I watched as he lifted his arm, and hurled the beer directly at mom, like a pitcher throwing the closing strike. The cans smashed into her head and shoulder. I was shocked, feet frozen to the floor. Mom rushed to the closet. Grabbing a baseball bat, she took a swing at him! My brain was taking in the scene; Mom was five feet four inches, and ninety-five pounds. Dad was a six foot tall ex-marine, weighing two hundred and fifteen pounds. He yanked the bat from her like a toy. I reached for it, but he jerked it away. Mom stepped between us.

He yanked the bat from her like a toy.

"Marlene, get away from him," she said through clenched teeth.

I hesitated. He took a swing at her. Instinct took over, and I shoved her out of the way. The bat connected squarely with my forehead. I do not know how long I was unconscious. I gingerly lifted up on my hands and feet, checking for blood and dizziness. I felt neither, but my legs were shaky.

"Mom? Dad?" No answer.

Fighting fear and dread, I glanced around the room, expecting to see her bloody body on the floor. They were both gone. The front door was wide open. I half crawled and half dragged myself to the door. It took a minute or two before I could stand. Stepping out the door, I listened for yelling, arguing, anything.

"MOM! *Oh, God, please let her be okay!* "Dad! Mom, where are you?"

In all the horrors of abuse and torture, this was the only time I thought, tonight someone might die!

Realizing this, I took off down the street to the house of a state trooper whose children I babysat. I screamed as loudly as possible, "He's going to kill her! Chris! Help!"

I ran up the steps and pounded on his front door.

"Please, wake up! He's going to kill her!" I shouted.

Chris opened the front door, and his wife Tracey pulled me inside, wrapping me in a blanket. "Marlene, what happened?"

I'm not sure how I answered, but he called the police. I wanted to go outside, but there was no way they were letting me. We soon heard sirens. The police chief came into the house, and brought an ambulance attendant with him. He did a quick assessment of me.

"You'll have a headache and a knot for a few days. If you have any other symptoms, go to your doctor," he smiled as he patted my arm. The Chief and Chris asked me a few questions. Dad's brother was on the City Council, so my last name ensured quick action. Spotlights, foot patrols, middle of the night searches, it read and looked like a television show. But it was playing out in real life...and it was my life. The search did not take long. A squad located dad walking home, arresting him on the spot. Mom was soon located in a culvert. The ambulance attendant treated her, but she insisted, "You have to go to my house! I think my daughter is dead!" Mom did not believe I was all right until she saw me.

After I was knocked out, dad went after her. She scrambled outside, crossing the street. He ran out with the bat in hand. He went down the street; she went across the field. He told police he threw the bat into the field as hard as he could. Dad spent the night in jail, but my uncle bailed him out, with a stern warning to behave. I never saw my uncle again, but dad was back home Sunday afternoon. The bat was never found.

I met my husband while I was in college. Jim and I were married on September 11, 1971. By November of 1978, we had two children. He was on a hunting trip, and I was home with our kids. The baby had an ear infection and screamed whenever I laid him down. I walked and rocked him for hours at a time, while occupying our two-year-old daughter. By five am the second morning, I was exhausted. When I put him in his crib, and he screamed again, a horrifying thought flashed through my mind, *if I throw him against the wall, he'll shut up*. I practically dropped him into the crib, and fled the room. I was ashamed and scared. I needed help. A friend was seeing a Christian counselor, and I made an appointment the next week.

> *I learned many things about my dad and me. I learned even more about my loving heavenly father.*

I learned many things about my dad and me. I learned even more about my loving, heavenly Father. After telling my counselor some long held secrets, he asked how I felt about being abused.

"It's been years since it happened. It was all pretty normal until near the end, and then I felt ashamed," I told him.

"You want to know how I feel about what happened to you?" he asked. Before I could answer, he slammed his fist on his desk, shouting, "MAD! I'm so angry that he did this to you!"

Anger was not something I felt. I was surprised anyone had feelings about my life. As I learned about the psychology of abuse, I read the Bible and prayed even more. I needed to hear God's voice on this. Reading words like forgiveness, kindness, and a love that never fails; I wondered how these feelings were possible. I needed to change, but didn't know how. I was a people pleaser who needed love. My hidden anger was a natural reaction to life. My overeating was an escape from feelings I didn't know I had. I did not discuss these feelings with anyone. Most people could not handle my story. I understood. I could barely handle my story, and I lived it. When I saw words like "forgive us as we forgive others" I was on to something. It took weeks to understand God was speaking to me about dad.

"Okay, Lord. I forgive my dad," I prayed.

God spoke to me…more kisses from heaven. God spoke in audible words; I've heard the voice of God a lot in my life, so it wasn't new. Gentle. Calm. It brings no fear. I never have a sense of just imagining His voice.

"I want you to face him, and tell him you forgive him. No lists, no accusations. Your only assignment is to let him know this, because I have called you out of darkness into My light. You forgive him for everything that happened."

I wasn't startled by His voice, just by what he asked me to do.

It was one thing to say, 'Okay, Lord, I forgive him,' but he was asking me to face him. That was new.

We can forgive someone who has offended us and it's between us and God; this was something different.

It felt like it would be a waste of time to do it; he would rage, maybe, or he wouldn't care at all, but I wasn't doing it for him.

"You mean…face to face? In person?" Swallowing hard, my whisper barely audible.

"Yes." I waited for more; I was waiting for Him to tell me what I was supposed to say. 'So what else?'

I sat there for thirty, forty minutes taking in what he told me to do, but God was waiting for me.

"Okay, Lord, I'll do what you ask. I'm going to need a LOT of help, Father."

"I will take you through."

God brought my heart to a place of accepting that my dad's response didn't matter…this was for me. It was a sense of laying down something that had held me captive for twenty-five years. My brother was getting married in a few months, and it would be the only time I would see my dad. I called and asked to meet him at the hotel an hour before the wedding.

A few months later, as Jim and I approached his hotel room, I paused. I needed to quiet my anxious thoughts.

What if he blows up?

What if he denies it?

What if I can't say it?

God, is this really You?

But I knew it was God. Turning to Jim, he reached out and held my arms. A quick smile, and reassurance, "You can do this. You know God has brought you here." I nodded, took a deep breath, and turned toward the room. I had asked Jim to sit on a bench outside and pray.

It was a nice hotel, but I sensed a darkness as I lifted my hand to knock. The interior door was open, and I heard a baseball announcer on television. There was a dark wood frame on the screen door, and the interior door was brown.

"Come on in," I heard Dad say. Three simple words, for most people they were welcoming. I felt slimed.

I could smell him before I saw him. Old Spice, he always wore it. It was still a trauma trigger. The memories caused me to insist my then boyfriend discontinue using it. I didn't know why, so I told Jim I didn't like the smell.

We had an agreed upon time, but Dad was on his own schedule. I glanced around the room and noticed his tuxedo hanging on the coat rack. It reminded me of an empty costume, waiting for its host to fill it with hot air.

I was grateful to breathe as memories were trying to infiltrate my resolve. He could always charm himself out of situations. I couldn't let him get to me today.

"So, how was your trip?" he asked, pulling on a clean tee shirt.

"It was good, thanks. And yours?" I replied.

"Mine was okay. What did you want to talk about?" he asked.

His get to the point abruptness startled me. It was just what I needed.

"Well, Dad, as you know, I became a Christian a number of years ago." I told him.

"I'm aware," he said, folding his arms across his chest.

"Well, I've been praying and thinking about all of the stuff between us. I want you to know that because of Who Christ is in me, I forgive you for all of it."

No pause. No consideration for what I just said.

"You mean, if it was just between us, you wouldn't forgive me?"

"If it was just between you and me, I would probably kill you."

> *If it was just between you and me, I would probably kill you.*

This is not what I was going to say. These words flew out of my mouth. My matter-of-fact statement hit him like a hammer. He took two unbalanced steps backwards, putting a hand shakily on the bed, as he quickly sat down.

I turned and left the room. I had no more to say to him. It was done. I had not thought about his response. Honestly, part of my expectation was that birds would start singing, forty pounds would drop off my body, and he would **finally** apologize and thank me for forgiving him. None of this happened.

Jim was waiting when I stepped into the fresh summer air. I had no tears. And my fear, which I had lived with for twenty-five years, was gone...just gone. All of those years filled with terror were over with one statement that was not planned. I had no idea what he would say after I told him why I was there.

My comment came from my heart. I knew who I would have been without Jesus. I knew I could have done it. Nothing will ever compare to the completeness of God's forgiveness and how truly free I had become in a moment.

A few months after the miracle, Dad called from an inpatient facility. He believed his own lies so much his doctor told him he could not have done those terrible things. Dad's call was designed to get me to retract what I said. Unbeknownst to me, his doctor was on an extension to hear me substantiate Dad's claims. It was the first time I was not bullied by him.

It felt so good to be free.

It felt so good to be free.

In my mid-twenties I learned Mom had sent me to Vacation Bible School when I was four. When I brought home an "I prayed the prayer" note, Mom knew I asked Jesus into my heart. This explained my closeness to God throughout my childhood. When I was free, I told God, "If you can use any of this, please do."

God said, "Okay."

As I began telling my story, a Women's Center asked me to counsel children and adult victims of childhood sexual abuse. Telling my secrets has brought more freedom and safety I ever believed possible. God has opened many doors for me to share and encourage others as He brings healing and freedom to all of us.

As a child I felt like I didn't fit anywhere. I was the new kid at school nearly every year. Just when I made friends, it was time to move again. While the geographic relocations were needed for protection, it was terrible to have no lasting friendships. Experiencing one incident of sexual abuse can lead to post traumatic stress disorder (PTSD), depression, self-hatred, and people pleasing, among other traumas. Fifteen years of abuse can warp many areas in one's life. By God's grace, I am better in most areas, but I still struggle. I've been accused of being plastic, having no feelings, and being too emotional and too connected. No one knows the lack of boundaries I've lived with, or known which lines to cross or not cross. But God had other plans. In the Bible, Revelation 2:17 (NIV) says, "Whoever has ears, let them hear what the Spirit says to the churches. To the one who [overcomes], I will give some of the hidden manna. I will also give that person a white stone with a new name written on it, known only to the one who receives it."

I was called fatso Finnegan, defeated, worthless, hopeless, loser, and many other names.

Now I am called HIS.

Reverend Billy Graham:

"The greatest legacy one can pass on to one's children and grandchildren is not money or other material things accumulated in one's life, but rather a legacy of character and faith."

LARA
LANDON

Lara Landon (www.laralandon.org) is a songwriter, worship leader, and author based out of Nashville, Tennessee. Whether she's meticulously crafting lyrics or playing for the physically and spiritually needy on nationwide tours that minister at prisons, rehabs, shelters, conferences, churches, and media outlets, authenticity reigns supreme. Having worked with Grammy Award winning writers and producers on seven albums, Lara maintains her main goal is to be an intermediary: "I'm a connector, and if I'm doing my part correctly, I will disappear and leave people face-to-face with their own heart and the heart of God." To find out more about Project 7, please visit: www.NewRealityInternational.org.

——— Chapter 3 ———

A KNOCK AT THE DOOR

Lara Landon

"He raises the poor from the dust and lifts the needy from the ash heap; he seats them with princes, with the princes of his people. He settles the childless woman in her home as a happy mother of children. Praise the Lord."

ᔕ *Psalm 113: 7-9 (NIV)*

By definition a miracle is "a surprising and welcome event that is not explicable by natural or scientific laws and is therefore considered to be the work of a divine agency." I simply call a miracle "a parting in the natural so the supernatural breaks in!" When God is performing such a breakthrough, sometimes all

39

we can do is stand back and watch it unfold with mouths dropped wide open!

I had the chance to be such a spectator when His supernatural plans all came together in a country not far from the U.S. but that seems a world away.

I was introduced to this land in 2009. A few years before, my sister Laila and I felt a passion to do something about the overwhelming problems in this world. The current reality of hunger, disease, poverty, and hopelessness was not the reality we wanted to see. One night as we talked, the name "New Reality" seemed fitting and our "organization" was born. We didn't know what exactly to do, so we decided to look around at what we had and use that. Her husband is a dentist that had been on many mission trips in school and even became a dentist just so he could do dental mission work. That seemed like a good place to start. Our trips started out very small, with just Laila and her husband, Joel, and some of his dentist friends. They traveled to Central America, carrying bags of dental supplies onto little planes and down river rafts to difficult to reach villages. We all used our own money to make these trips work. Laila diligently pursued this dream, getting the right paperwork done to become a non-profit, writing grants, recruiting help, and planning trips. We see now that God was stretching us, letting us learn by trial and error and preparing us for the rescue He was about to unfold!

In 2009 God tugged on our hearts to venture into Haiti. Even though the plane ride from Florida to Haiti is only a few hours, it's a different world entirely. This was before the earthquake that brought Haiti into the world's focus. I'd actually never even heard of Haiti as we prepared to go. As I did research, I found myself wondering how the people would act and if they would welcome us. I'd read much about the voodoo practices and witchcraft that was prevalent throughout Haiti.

My fears were not alleviated when we arrived at the chaotic Port Au Prince airport. Men were fighting over our bags, so they would get the tip. I was overwhelmed with the yelling and foreign smells everywhere. Trash covered the streets and the smell of burning tires made me almost nauseous. We rode to the mission we'd be based at in the open bed of a dilapidated truck. The pot holes in the roads were infamous in Haiti and I felt every one as we bounced down the road for about an hour in the sun. Motorcycles zoomed by, intersections seemed to have no order. Women with baskets on their heads walked the sides of dusty streets or sat on the ground selling fruit. When we arrived at the mission, Betty, our host was warm and welcoming. Shady trees hung near a beautiful where veranda where children looked down at us smiling curiously. The gates closed behind us at the peaceful property and I felt a sense of total calm.

In the days that followed I fell in love with the people of Haiti, particularly the precocious children. I even wrote a song called "I See God In You" about one of the mentally handicapped boys I bonded with there. I loved Haitians for their laid back demeanor and sense of humor. After long hot days of acting as a "dental assistant" cleaning, disinfecting and then preparing new trays of dental tools for the hundreds of people we would see, we would relax in the evenings by singing worship songs and playing card games on the cool veranda with the kids. The kids clung to us, poking and touching our foreign faces. Their giggles and smiles were infectious. We became particularly close to our translators and they took us to the beach to see the natural beauty of Haiti. I loved the coffee and bananas each morning and rice, beans and red sauce served to us at night. One day you'd see a bony chicken pecking around the yard. The next day it would be added to the red sauce as a treat! I felt like I had found a home among the team and the children, working and eating together. It was hard to leave them.

I remember remarking to my sister as we surveyed the whole city of Port Au Prince from a lookout mountain, "These buildings don't look stable; they look like they could just crumble on top of each other. I hope an earthquake never happens here." I was horrified when a few months later I turned on the news and saw the devastation the great earthquake had caused. I tried frantically to find out how my new friends were. Some who we knew, some that had helped us as translators and drivers, were crushed and died. I thought of the children, what would happen to them?

The nation of Haiti was born in struggle. The Spanish, French, and countless others dominated and plundered the rich land of this island, until the native people established their own rule in 1934. These resilient people then came under the most oppressive regime with the infamous "Papa Doc" and "Baby Doc" his son, dictators who were said to have called upon satanic forces for their own gain, while sending the nation into utter poverty. Just like the nation itself, many children in Haiti are born into struggle.

The name "Restevek" is given to children whose families are so poor, they send these children to work in other households that can house and feed them. Restevek children, sometimes as young as five years old, are made to fetch water, cook, clean, are often abused sexually, physically and verbally and given inadequate nutrition. Two out of ten children in Haiti would fall under this category of "Restevek." If that wasn't a problem enough, after the devastating earthquake in 2010 matters only got worse.

Now, orphaned children roamed the streets, looking for shelter, food, and the ability to survive.

At just that point, where the situation seemed beyond repair, God stepped in. He had always been with the vibrant believers in Haiti. I witnessed, first hand, their remarkable faith and devotion to God as believers gathered in bare bone churches and sang praises until the wee hours of the morning. I saw Haitians helping one another and smiling their huge, welcoming smiles as they waited patiently for long hot hours in line for medical care.

We'd witnessed many amazing ways God arranged and aligned for our teams to go in before and after the earthquake and help many hundreds of desperate people, forge friendships and be inspired by their humility and joy, but the story I'm about to tell, is nothing short of a certifiable miracle.

Near the port town of Porte Au Prince a new believer in God, a young man name Frantz, had just gotten baptized. The day after his baptism, God awoke him before dawn and told him clearly "Go to the orphanage in Trou du Nord and help them." Frantz didn't know anyone in the northern part of the country, where Trou Du Nord was located and didn't have money for the long bus fare through the mountains but he asked his friend to help him scrape together money, and he set out. He arrived tired and hungry, to a village he had never even heard of before God spoke to him that morning. He felt so strongly this strange request had to be from the Lord.

Meanwhile, a group of seven adult believers had been taking in orphans since 2001 in Trou Du Nord. Out of their own poverty, they gathered money to find a shack with a dirt floor and leaky roof to house the kids, and each of the seven, would take turns feeding them. After the ravage of the earthquake more orphaned and Restevek kids roamed the streets, they felt compassion to try to take them all in. At the same time the earthquake caused a surge in food prices so some days, there would be no food at all. They would boil water and add salt to give the kids something hot to fill their bellies. There is an old saying "when there is no food to eat, it's time to fast." That is what this group of desperate people did. These seven elders decided to pray and fast with the children for seven days. They needed God to break in supernaturally and provide for them or they might literally die.

As Frantz walked through True Du Nord, asking where the orphanage was, people pointed him to the shack. It was the seventh day of the fast, and there was a knock on the door.

> Everyone thought
> God had sent food
> and provision.

The kids jumped up in excitement! Everyone thought God had sent food and provision, but to their surprise Frantz asked them if they had anything to eat! He had absolutely nothing to give them, except the word that God had sent him there that day. But, there was one thing that he could try to do for them after hearing their story. He thought of an Australian woman he had translated for named Cay. He called her and explained the situation and immediately her heart was touched. Cay jumped on a flight without delay. Within days the kids were in a new place she rented for them. Still no running water, but at least it didn't have a dirt floor. Most importantly, they now had food! She even gave enough to start sending some of the kids to school.

This group of seven had a vision of housing many children since they came together in 2001. They prayed to God and asked the government for land to build an orphanage. They dreamed of giving kids land where they could play soccer, have a garden, clean water and safety. Without any resources

at all, they kept praying and knew with God maybe one day it would be possible.

Cay, the Australian lady who rushed in to help, had met my sister Laila, in the airport on the way to Port Au Prince. But they had lost touch for many years. Laila and the team had been praying about what projects to take on as there was so much need and many people asked us to help with their efforts in Haiti. None of these opportunities felt quiet right so we kept praying. As Laila was on a anti-human trafficking tour in Australia, she was invited to a church service, and the person serving communion looked strangely familiar. It was Cay. The rejoiced in finding each other so randomly after so much time had passed. Cay filled Laila in on what her and her small church were doing to support the orphans in True Du Norde. They were barely able to keep the children somewhat housed and fed, but they were nowhere near being able to build them the dream that the seven elders had: the dream of a beautiful orphanage on their own land. Laila felt in her spirit this was the project we needed to be a part of. Through more fasting and prayer, with Cay, Laila, and our team, the government gave the elders seven acres of land to build the orphanage. Because of the seven elders, the seven days of fasting that brought Frantz to them, and the seven acres of land, we named this building project "Project 7."

Now the dream is a reality for the elders and thirty children we've come to know and love. We don't call it an "Orphanage," as these kids are no longer orphans. They are adopted into a family now. We call this place a "Children's Village" and it truly is a safe haven for these precious ones who've endured so much. The kids are safe within a wall that was built around the property, they have a full time cook, a well with fresh water, loving house parents, and they attend school, tend the garden and play soccer.

Could this have come about any other way than God's hand reaching down to orchestrate just the right meetings at just the right times? As I reflect on this great miracle of

> *God used seemingly powerless people...to accomplish His plans.*

provision that I witnessed firsthand, I'm struck by how God used seemingly powerless people and orphaned children's prayers to accomplish His plans. He truly is a father to the fatherless and will not let one sparrow fall to the ground unnoticed.

Countless miracles are happening every day, but we get to take part in them when we open ourselves to the miracles. The Bible says "If you spend yourselves on behalf of the hungry and satisfy the needs of the oppressed, then your light will rise in the darkness, and your night will become like the noonday." Isaiah 58:10

When these whirlwinds of awe inspiring chain of events occur, it increases our faith and gives us a testimony of just what kind of wonders our God can perform! I will never forget how he scooped up these children, just as a Father would, and showed his undeniable presence in all of our lives. The supernatural definitely broke in to save these kids and it broke in to show me the power and mercy of God.

Today thirty children, some whom would have been household slaves, are living under the protection and care of trusted care givers, receiving an education and even learning trades and working in the garden. Today, the miracle of God bringing together just the right people and resources is still unfolding.

Beth Moore:

"Faith is not believing in my own unshakable belief. Faith is believing an unshakable God when everything in me trembles and quakes."

TRACY
HENNES

With eighteen years of experience as a speech-language pathologist, *Tracy Hennes* has a firm belief in the power of communication and sharing stories. She is a small business owner who combines her faith, values, and passion for natural health and wellness, with her drive and desire to help others. Tracy is a certified Holy Yoga Instructor, member of the Yoga Alliance, and is studying Trauma-Sensitive Holy Yoga. She enjoys quality time with her three children and her husband in their Wisconsin home, tweaking recipes, hiking, and working out in fun t-shirts! Please visit: tracyhennes.com.

——— Chapter 4 ———

WARRIOR

Tracy Hennes

"And after you have suffered a little while, the God of all grace, who has called you to his eternal glory in Christ, will himself restore, confirm, strengthen, and establish you."

๑ 1 Peter 5:10 (ESV)

The pain and shame of a weary warrior who has wrestled with life…that's what I saw as I took a brief look at my reflection over the row of brightly lit porcelain bowls. I peered closer and ran my fingertips across the soft, deep creases across my forehead. My massaging effort to fight their invasion upon my face was pointless.

As I straightened up to leave, I noticed *her* reflection next to mine. She was about my mom's age with a glowing complexion and a gloriously smooth plane above her eyes. Her face told me a story of her life of peace, joy, and abundance (either that or she slept in a top-secret formula like those women who sell makeup and facial products). Whatever her story, I was instantaneously perturbed. She warmly smiled at me, and we followed each other out into the filtered sunlit sea of beautiful Christian women gathered for the conference. In her white and floral chiffon blouse paired with crisp, white skinny jeans, she floated over to her friends and then disappeared into the crowd. I looked down, and felt like the villain of the story, wearing black skinny jeans and a silky blouse that resembled the colors of a severe bruise. *I don't belong here*, was the thought running through my head. My battle wounds are deep, and even if I had the perfect floral blouse, it could not hide the fact that I am no angel, like these women appeared to be. *Perhaps this wounded warrior should retreat to her car?* Then a friend grabbed my arm and pulled me in the direction of the mob. There was no turning back. *Take a deep breath and grab your shield, Tracy, I said to myself.*

> My battle wounds are deep.

Have you ever taken a good look in the mirror and wondered, *How in the heck did I end up here?* Do you see your image and realize the many flaws you have to hide and cover up so you can fit in or feel a little better about yourself? Are you open, honest, content, or feel the need to conceal, strategize, and fight for your place in society? As an idealist, I can tell you that I've never been content. I perpetually strive for better. As thoughts of being unworthy or burdensome continually claim their ground in the battlefield of my mind, I fight for myself or for others in an effort to feel like I have a rightful place in this world. You could ask my husband, my three children, friends, and extended family about it; many appreciate me taking up my sword for others, but those closest to me are often concerned that I say "yes," too often for my own good. The lifetime of battles I've taken upon myself, the walls I've built, the shields I've held up, the battle cries that run through my head...they've all taken their toll and have left their marks. Then one fateful spring day at the women's conference my heavenly Father, my chief and commander, wanted to be sure I heard His miracle message for me, His "marching orders," and to know what He sees in me. My battles would never be the same.

He counts the stars and calls them all by name. –Psalm 147:4

Warrior, war-like, bold, brave, fighter...these are all meanings associated with *Tracy*. It is my name and the role I've taken on since before I even knew my name had a meaning; actually before I even took my first breath. My mom told me I was born purple, not breathing, and the umbilical cord was wrapped around my neck. My young mother didn't know the meaning of my name when she gave it to me, but at first sight she knew I wasn't meant to be "Jennifer," the name she and my dad had picked out. Knowing that I had to fight to live, I believe God chose my name and put it on my mom's heart to utter it into existence. *Tracy*. A born *fighter*; that's me. It's who my heavenly father created me to be, but this was at odds with my upbringing. We were to be quiet, respectful, and obey. I was often told, "no tattling," and "don't talk back." I was taught to be responsible, independent, and careful not to talk about politics, money, relationships, or subjects that could be upsetting or controversial. We attended Sunday mass at our church where we followed the routines, recited the prayers, and listened to the priest interpret the readings from the Bible. I usually left church feeling like our congregation had just received a scolding instead of an inspiration. I grew to dislike church, especially when I had to look only a couple pews behind me each week to see that face, the face of my abuser. I would see those big, dark brown eyes and felt far greater shame than that which the priest was already preaching to us from his pulpit.

I was just a little girl when the period of abuse happened. It was sexual and psychological in nature. The abuser was not a family member, but a local member of our church whom my parents had entrusted me with for periods of time. The perpetrator told me, "This is what everybody does." I was also directed to not talk about it with anyone, "because it would make my parents and other people mad." I did as I was told. The only visible reminder of the "under the blanket games" that occurred in my parents absence was the burnt circle on one of my blankets. I grew to hate that blanket. I remember feeling an angry satisfaction the day I saw the black circle forming on it as the heat from the bulb of the table lamp started to sear its way through the fabric. I hated the way that blanket smelled and how just the sight of it could make me feel sick to my stomach. My mother had made that blanket for me. It was supposed to be special. *How could I have let that happen?* Then came shame. My young and formative psyche could not handle the trauma of it all, and I blocked the memories for a few years.

I was in seventh or eighth grade when I had my first crush. There were joyful schoolgirl giggles in classes as a few of us passed small, white, folded sheets of paper with question marks and check boxes in an effort to harness the energy and figure out, *does he like me too?* He did like me. All he had to do was smile at me with those warm blue eyes and the butterflies stirred in my stomach as my cheeks started to feel warm. Along with the joy, and excitement there was confusion and darkness; memories of something familiar, but different. Recollections of the abuse came back slowly at first, but then it seemed like a tidal wave of flashbacks complete with smells, sounds, feelings, an overwhelming sense of shame and embarrassment, all hit me at once. I wanted these memories to disappear. I'd seen the specials on TV that told stories of the abusive parent grabbing a child so hard, she'd get bruises on her arm. *Why couldn't I have had normal abuse like that?* Normal abuse...two words that should not be used together. It's not what God had intended for any of us.

Promise me, O women of Jerusalem, not to awaken love until the time is right. - Song of Songs 8:4

God knew what He was doing when he breathed these words of warning into the Bible. The confusing pubescent teen years filled with a changing body, hormones, new friends, phone calls from teenage boys, peer pressure, and sexuality being awakened before its time was such a mess for me. *How could I have let myself be ruined like that? How can I fix this, replace the memories, dull the pain?* I had no idea how to deal with boys pursuing me or the emotions that I would start to have toward a boyfriend. I had simultaneous love-hate feelings when I was at football games, dances, and parties. I loved being around the joyful energy of my teenage friends, but at the same time I hated myself. Alcohol seemed to make it all easier. I could forget, at least temporarily. Then I started to replace the memories of those childhood sexual encounters with newly found teen sexual promiscuity. I still hated myself enough that I'd usually end the relationship quickly, especially if it was with a nice guy. At the same time, I desperately wanted to feel loved.

I was seventeen. He could make me laugh and help me to forget the cruddy things in life like nobody else. He was the "bad boy" with the killer smile. Everybody liked him. I thought it was real love, but he mistreated me, lied to me, and hid his real self from me. Looking back, I realize now he was just a teenager dealing with his own hurts, but I wanted him to love me forever. I was willing to do whatever it took to keep him.

"Are you buckled up?" he asked as he looked over at me from the driver's seat. The smile that could make everything seem okay was nowhere to be found today. His gaze followed my hands as I snapped the seatbelt into place. He put the car in drive, and we pulled away from my parents' house as they watched out the window. As we started towards the clinic in Milwaukee, my vision blurred to a cloudy gray and the tears seemed to cling to my eyelashes. I couldn't see in front of me, but I could hear the events and thoughts of the last few days replaying in my head...*there's a fetus...there's something wrong...but I'm on the pill...we can't tell how far along you are...but I'm on the pill...do you want to terminate the pregnancy? We're here for you...you have a choice...you can apply for a loan to help you cover the cost... How many times did you drink? Did you do any drugs? Is riding a roller coaster harmful to a fetus? How could I have let this happen?* It was all so confusing. *He said he wanted this, right? Why is this the first time he cared if I had my seatbelt on or not?*

The mind is a funny thing, with infinite capacities science has yet to fully understand, but in the face of trauma, self-protection can kick in and the memory is erased. God made our bodies. He created our minds. He made it possible to protect us from the horrible traumas of this human life by being able to effectively erase and block out traumatic events, but the scars and lessons remain. What I remember next was lying in my twin bed at home, recovering; no longer pregnant.

> *(God) made it possible to protect us from the horrible traumas of this human life.*

I didn't feel relief.

I felt empty...alone...ashamed.

I felt like God was mad at me, and I now had a debt with Him that was so large, it could never be fixed. I imagined dying, right then and there in my bed. Like the scene from the movie, *Ghost*, when evil Carl's soul is dragged to hell. I imagined my death and fate would look the same; the black, screaming and moaning silhouettes of the demons dragging me away into the darkness. No more golden gates or choir of angels for me. *How could I have let this happen?*

For I know the plans I have for you, declares the Lord, plans to prosper you and not to harm you, plans to give you hope and a future. –Jeremiah 29:11

The sunlit room was behind me now as I was being swept with the mob through the double doors. The waves in the sea of women seemed to break apart quickly as they drifted into row after row after row of seating. The large auditorium was modern, decorated with screens, banners, sparkles and all things "girly" for what looked to be an impressive party. Upbeat Christian music played in the background. I followed our small tribe into a row and breathed a sigh of relief at being able to take the aisle seat; *a quick escape route if necessary.* We all looked through our swag bags, some showed off the bracelets or books they had bought at the waiting area boutiques. I'm a note taker, so in anticipation of our first speaker, I eagerly grabbed the pen and the small booklet for notes from inside the bag. "Write Your Story" was displayed across the cover of the blank journal. *It's a shame I really can't use this to write my story. I sealed my own fate 25 years ago and God has every right to be mad at me.* I thought about the tribe to my right; a mixed bag of women, some friends for over a decade others very new to me. Just like everyone, no matter how long they'd been in my life, *none of these women really knows my story.*

Lively and moving Christian song performances set the tone for the evening, followed by announcements of what was to come. A young pastor's wife, impeccably dressed in an outfit complete with a flowy, sheer, floral duster gave an inspiring talk about our imperfections and how we are all still absolutely beautiful and worthy in God's eyes. Then one of my favorite Christian women, an author and speaker with a great sense of humor, down-to-earth style, and an endearing ability to laugh at herself, lead a presentation that seemed so inspired it was supernatural. During her talk, she admitted to having an abortion. *Did I hear that right? How did I not know this?!* I tried hard not to react. I didn't want anybody to be able to read the look on my face and guess my own dark secret. I was so glad I had been recording her speech with my phone so I could listen again on the way home. I was sure I had misunderstood her. She must have been talking about someone else. A small group of women were brought onto the stage and told their stories of pregnancies terminated and how God was now in control and writing their stories. Their life stories were of joy, forgiveness, and purpose. *Really, God, are you trying to torture me? The happy ending to the story isn't meant for me. They may be worthy, but I am not.* I had only said it in my head, but God heard me and He was not going to be okay with that! I didn't know what was happening, but I can tell you that my senses were suddenly heightened.

As the master of ceremonies for the evening held the microphone in front of her, the quiet murmur of women talking around me turned into silence. The darkness of the room was cut by the spotlight shining on the emcee, but I could no longer see her and there was a blinding glare bouncing back at me. It was shining right into my face. I felt self-conscious, afraid; there was no place to hide. The purse hanging across my hip, felt like the weight of an anchor, holding me in place. It kept me grounded. (I reached for it to make sure I was feeling correctly and still had my senses about me.) There was a Kleenex hanging out of the partially opened top zipper. My eyes began to water, and I let my fingers rest on the tissue, just in case. I could hear myself sniffling, and held back the fluids that would surely fall. I was embarrassed. *Please don't let the women next to me hear me sniffling. Be strong!* Then a loud, clear, voice, bellowed, **"God's not mad at you!"** *Who's she talking to?* I sensed a camera man moving forward from my back left side, upward into the aisle. I could hear his footsteps getting louder and I was suddenly super self-conscious that my left arm was raised toward the light. *I'm a freak. Oh please don't see me. Please don't* *put me on a camera. Let me shrink back into the shadows.* The salty taste of tears intermingled with sugary sweet taste of a breath mint I had earlier. The clashes of salty and sweet, light and dark, quiet and loud, good and evil...it felt like a thunder storm and the air felt absolutely electrified. I was drawn into the moment again. The voice repeated, more loudly and more clearly than the first time, **"God's not mad at you!"** There was no mistaking it that time. The message *was* for me. I was almost afraid to think what a third time would have felt like. I let myself settle in. Tears and snot flowed. Thankfully, I was in the dark again and I could wipe it up and try to collect myself.

"Ladies, if you feel you really received Jesus and heard God's message for you, we invite you to come forward after the crowd is dismissed. We want to pray for you and we have a gift for you. There are also staffed prayer rooms off of the main gathering area for you, if you'd like someone to pray with," said the emcee. She was wrapping up the event in the auditorium now and verbally steering the crowd to the next venue for food, music, and community gathering. I felt frozen in place and horribly conflicted. *What if my friends see I've been crying, and I walk forward to that stage? Will they wonder if I've been a phony at our church all along? Will they worry about my salvation? Will they think I'm a freak? Abandon me? And she talked about a gift...God, I don't want a gift. I don't deserve one. Please don't make me go up there.* It felt like every little hair on my body was pulling me toward the front of the room, but I fought it. It felt like swimming against a strong river current as I made my way with the tribe. The words that came from their mouths felt annoying, trivial; it literally hurt to listen. My husband called and was upset about something on the phone. His words shook me. I made the call brief. God was calling to me all the while. I fought it. The tribe slowly made their way toward the next area of the building. As I got farther from the auditorium, I felt physically ill from the force pulling me in the other direction, like when a roller coaster takes you in reverse. There was a point where I couldn't take it anymore.

I turned to a friend and said, "I can't explain it, but I feel like I have to go to one of those prayer rooms and pray with somebody."

Concerned that I was upset about my husband's phone call, she asked, "Would you like me to come with you?"

"No, I've got this." I was always ready to fight my battles on my own.

I was always ready to fight my battles on my own.

As I found my way to a prayer room, the awful weight on my body started to lessen. The prayer room stood in stark contrast to the space I'd just left. Outside the door it was bright and busy. As the door was shut, I could see this room was very plain: windows around the top of the undecorated walls, a couple of chairs, kind of brown. There was not much to really feel or sense there other than the words that would be spoken. "I don't know why I'm here, just that I need to be here," I said to the woman who had warmly greeted me.

She took a second before beginning.

Growing up in a Catholic family, I didn't spend a lot of time in the Bible, myself. In my childhood churches, only the priest would touch the Bible. We would hold books that had only specific and chosen parts in it for our services. At home, we owned a big, white Bible and it sat on a shelf in a special place. Opening the Bible and digging into the Word was new for me, but I had just learned about Paul, his history of persecuting followers of Jesus, and how he had been converted and became one of the most prevalent writers in the Bible. I had also learned about the armor of God. Because the bible was so new to me, there wasn't a whole lot from scripture that I could relate to at that time. I didn't know what this moment of prayer would be like.

The prayer began.

"I feel like God is telling me," she began as she touched my head, "I feel like, when it comes to that helmet from the armor of God, you need to stop letting your own head get in the way."

As she touched my head, I felt a warm-cool rush start at the top of my body and go all the way down to my toes.

How did she know? How did she know of the few verses I was familiar with and that I'd spent way too much time in my own head? The next day, when I saw the same woman who prayed with me again, she didn't even recollect the words she used. Those words were clearly from God. (Even today, as I write of this experience, God's giving me confirmation. I just now discovered that Paul's conversion came during a blinding light and was accompanied by the voice of Jesus!?)

Looking back on that sunny May day, I wish I could tell you I was instantly obedient. That was over two years ago now, and what I've learned and loved most about God through this process is how He may nudge and guide, but he will not push. He gave me free will and it's taken a while for this warrior to lower her shield. I've learned to open my eyes, my ears, my heart, and my senses.

There have been messages and signs from Him frequently, all telling me, "God's not mad at you," and "You are a daughter of the King of all Creation. Step into that. Straighten your crown, throw your shoulders back, and take up your sword for the right battles. Be who you were designed to be."

I'm still a warrior at heart, but my battles are now against the enemy who wants us to believe lies. I am a fighter because God wants each and every one of us to live in the light; not the darkness. I take back the ground from the enemy, and I'm here to share the Good News that it is possible for you. I now wield the Word and weave it into my daily routines and practices. I fight battles alongside others, helping them to worship God with heart, soul, mind, and strength. God is not mad at any of us. Stop believing lies and start living His Truth.

When I look in the mirror: yes, I see the lines. They remind me of the stress and heaviness I unnecessarily put my soul under for years, but I had to wander in that desert to prepare. I've now straightened my path, put my priorities in order, and have allowed the warmth of His love to shine upon my face. I would take on another wrinkle if it meant that I had broken another chain of lies. After all, I am a daughter of the King of all Creation, and He is not mad at me.

Joyce Meyer:

"No matter what you have gone through or might be going through right now, you can hope (have faith) that God is working on your behalf right now and you will see the results of His work in your life. You don't have to be a prisoner of your circumstances, but instead you can be a prisoner of hope!"

TARA

JOHNSON-

BROWER

Tara Johnson-Brower is a wife and mom of two boys residing in Grand Rapids Michigan. People who know Tara would refer to her as a true servant leader. Tara's faith is unshakable and her mission in life is to add value to others, which she does on a daily basis. Her hunger for success is matched by few in her industry; however "success" to Tara is not a dollar amount, but instead the number of hearts she has impacted. She desires to be a small part of someone else's success story. You may follow Tara at www.johnsonbrower.com.

—— Chapter 5 ——

GOD CHOSE ME

Tara Johnson-Brower

"Finally, be strong in the Lord and in his mighty power. Put on the full armor of God, so that you can take your stand against the devil's schemes."

∾ Ephesians 6:10-11 (NIV)

Have you ever used humor to somewhat mask the devastation that's going on inside? You know that saying: "Laughter is the best medicine?" I am here to tell you that it works!

When I look back on different events in my husband's and my life together, it has become clear to me why God created my husband, Jesse, with an unbelievably funny sense of humor. He can make anyone laugh! Studies show that laughter reduces pain and allows us to tolerate discomfort. There was a lot of discomfort in our home, but a whole lotta laughter!

It was a beautiful night. I had dimmed the lights to start our nighttime routine. The water in our kitchen sink was the perfect temperature for my sweet, three month old, Taggan. We were buddies, as Jesse worked diligently to build his gym from the ground up. You see, this was his third poke at a job since we began our marriage two years prior. God has blessed him with a creative, entrepreneurial brain and, for some reason, he hated working for employers. At the time I didn't know why.

Bath time. You know that feeling as a mom when you're on schedule; your baby is fed and now your baby will be squeaky clean. I still remember those feelings like that night was yesterday. A knock quickly diminished those feelings as I looked toward our front door. **Fear stole the color from my face as I saw two grown men standing in the dark.** I quickly grabbed Taggan and wrapped him in his hooded towel. Walking hesitantly to the door, I felt very uncertain of what to do and if I should answer, but there was no turning back as they both stared at me through the window. Holding my sweet baby boy, I opened the door: "What can I help you guys with?" I asked timidly with fear on my face.

"Ma'am, we're with the bank, and we're here to take your car," said the strange men.

My stomach literally dropped, my ears started ringing, and it was like the world was in slow motion. With panic in my voice, I asked, "What do you mean you're here to take my car?! I don't understand!"

"Ma'am, we are the repo (repossession) guys. We've sent warnings," they demanded.

My mind started spinning as I looked down at my precious son who no doubt could feel my fear and panic. As they walked toward my garage I quickly lay Taggan down. I realized his car seat was in my car. "Wait! Please wait! Would you please give me a few minutes to get my son's car seat out?" I begged desperately.

My heart raced as I quickly fumbled over trying to unbuckle his car seat while the two strange men stood over me. There I stood in shock at the door, holding my son who was still wrapped in his hooded bath towel, as my car was taken away. *Repossessed.*

So many emotions came over me as I frantically tried to get hold of Jesse at the gym. I was so upset that I remember shaking while trying to breastfeed Taggan to sleep that night.

You see, I have trust issues…major trust issues, and thoughts ran through my head: *Was I clueless? How did I have no idea that we were behind on bills? How am I going to get my car back? Was I spending too much? Wait, I was hardly spending any money.*

Jesse had always been a jump now and ask for forgiveness later kind of person. This was one of those times. I felt he knew this was coming, as he was abnormally calm that night. He tried to explain that everything would be okay and attempted to convince me not to worry. I'm forever grateful for my parents, as my mom picked Taggan and me up a couple days later for an hour-long car ride to "buy" my car back. During this journey, my parents were our real life-saving grace. They showed us Christ's Love many times through the ways that they guided and helped us. The day we were able to pay them back was refreshing…so refreshing.

My husband, Jesse, is an Army Ranger Veteran. There was a time before we dated when I thought this dude was crazy…seriously. But there was something about him; our connection was deep; God-ordained deep. There was a gentleness when I looked into his green eyes. I always had a feeling there was so much more to him, but his sense of humor would often hide his vulnerability. We fell madly in love and exchanged vows: lifetime, unconditional vows. I was used to working and providing so it wasn't new to me when I had to be the steady income earner. I just should've known there was more to it, though. There were so many signs that there was more going on below the surface. Usually I can pick up on those things but I think the busyness of being new parents jaded my ability to read the situation.

Jesse was always so calm and brought humor when yet another job didn't work out. We look back and laugh over the fact that we once celebrated when he was employed for eleven months. I remember saying, "Oh my word, you're almost at a full year with the same job!" Then, just before the year mark, he quit.

The question, *'Is this normal?'* rang through my mind on a regular basis, but—to us—this *was* our normal. You see, I knew our marriage was different, but *I was missing the clarity of why.* You know any of those "faith like a child" people? That's me. I've always had faith like a child; I never questioned anything God relayed. I just trusted and believed. That seems pretty funny to me because, as I shared, I have trust issues. That's my thing, I have a difficult time trusting, but my trust in the Lord has never wavered. Maybe that's why one of my first tattoos read: "Trust in the Lord." Yes; I'm the girl who loves God hard and I have tattoos…many tattoos…figure that one out!

Have you taken the spiritual gift test? I have taken a couple of different ones and discernment is my strongest by far. *Discernment: the ability to obtain sharp perceptions or the process of determining God's desire in a situation.* I can tell you that my radar was flashing; wait, it was more like a bright, red-orange flare, but I didn't know what to do. The weight of finances, being a new mom, owning my own salon, extended family troubles, and a husband who was lost, was so heavy that it felt suffocating at times. In all of this, Jesse was so lost, but so likable, funny, and mentally strong, that I just couldn't figure it out. It wasn't like me; I can usually figure out things.

It was a Thursday evening just before dinnertime when the pieces were finally starting to fit together. Taggan, who was eighteen months old, and Jesse were playing in the living room; they seriously were two peas in a pod. I was in the loft on the computer when I saw it...one email that would change our worlds. My hand immediately covered my mouth as I gasped for a breath that was sucked out of me. My shaky legs carried my three months' pregnant body down the steep stairs, while I processed how to go about talking to Jesse about this.

'How is this possible? How could he have hidden this from me? Should I act upset or try to be calm? Holy cow! Is this really happening?'

I walked into our cozy living room with the computer in my hands. The smell of dinner cooking almost made me sick, but the noise of the television in the background seemed to oddly help me from panicking. I tried to smile at the two of them playing so sweetly together but my face wouldn't move. I was completely numb. He looked up at me and could read it all over my face.

"What's wrong babe?" He said it with such concern, which is not like him. I still wonder if he was just waiting for this day to come.

"Um, we got an email." I said as he quickly stood up. "Joe Smith[1] sent an email to you at our family email address."

Joe had to email our family address because Jesse had decided to abruptly close his fitness gym down that past October and—with it—his email phone number. Actually, when I thought about it, he went through nine different phone numbers and never set up a voicemail. That should have been another clue; I just wasn't educated in all of this…yet.

The mention of Joe Smith's name did something physically to Jesse right before my eyes. Time and the world stopped, and everything moved in super slow motion. I watched him go from red, to even brighter red, then as pale as a crisp white sheet while he backed up and fell into the chair behind him. Was it relief? Relief that the "secret" was out? Or was it truth slapping him in the face along with the fact that he was now going to have to work through this instead of continuing to shove it down to survive?

Whatever it was, I'm just grateful that time seemed to stop as it brought me clarity. So much clarity. As I slowly looked down at the email, memories crashed over me like a wild river. No wonder he couldn't keep a job. No wonder he's had nights with no sleep, only to wake up in the garage after sleepwalking. No wonder he starts sweating when Taggan cries. No wonder why he's been drinking at night…every night. No wonder he's lost contact with friends. No wonder he wants nothing to do with God. No wonder, when I ask him to tell me Army stories while I try to fall asleep, all he talks about are

So much clarity.

———————————————

[1] *Name changed to protect privacy.*

funny stories. Remember, it is said that laughter reduces pain and allows us to tolerate discomfort.

I timidly started asking him questions about the stats that I was reading from the email. As I asked him about this thing called a JSOC team that he was on, he lifted his finger to show me the tattoo. Got it, so that's what that tattoo really symbolized.

Did he really serve in nine combat deployments to Iraq, six to Afghanistan, and once to Africa? He shook his head. I asked him if he remembered how few men were on his team and the many that were killed in action. He nodded. I just stood there and stared at him while my eyes filled up with tears...so many details in one email. Any time I would mention his service, he would blow it off so quickly and only talk about two different combat deployments, not sixteen. The email came after his captain, along with two others, had taken their own lives. They couldn't manage another day after what they'd had to do and see.

As I continued to gently ask questions, the different emotions on his face started to paint a picture, a picture that made me aware that this was just the beginning of a new emotional journey. Then, it hit me. It hit me, not like a ton of bricks, but rather more like fresh rain hitting my face...an awakening feeling.

God chose me. He chose me!

All of the different things I battled through in the past had created an unshakable steadfastness; an unbreakable perseverance to battle through this thing called post-traumatic stress disorder (PTSD), resulting from Jesse's military combat. While the fresh rain was hitting my face, all of pieces started coming together like a messy, beautiful puzzle. So many questions of why Jesse had been doing what he was doing and acting like he was acting were finally answered through reading the devastatingly astounding stats from the email that Thursday in March. That night I felt convicted: convicted to fight for my husband and fight for our life together.

The next few months, while waiting for the (gratefully, healthy) arrival of our sweet Briggs, I saw what the affects of PTSD from military combat could do. Was it a blessing that his stats and story came out, or would he rather have tucked it away for the rest of his life? Hearing of the hallucinations he was having, the cold sweats, the drinking, the drug use, the raw emotions and memories which made him physically ill; and the vomiting was difficult. He had dreams so real that he could smell and taste war. This was all so hard to watch and manage at times, but God chose me. It *was* gut-wrenching, but God chose me. I trusted God fully, like the little girl swinging who trusts her daddy's first underdog.

Along with God, I surrounded myself with a sounding board: People I trusted, people who would realize we had a different dynamic, but would be okay with it, and people who could keep our lives to themselves. My parents were and are an amazing strength for us. My dad is an active listener; he listens...fully listens, and is careful to respond in a very gentle, yet clear way. My mom? Well, she loves hard, would give you the shirt off her back, and isn't afraid to say and show her true emotion. I needed them oh so much in the beginning of this journey, and I still need them, often. And, what would I have done without my cousin Jamie? I could be real with her and I knew she wouldn't judge me. Better yet, I knew the idea of her telling me to leave him would never enter her mind or mouth. She was a safe place for me. When it was bad, she wouldn't hesitate picking up a call from me late in the night while I sat outside and vented.

One night, though, was especially different. I use the word "different" because I still don't truly know how to express my feelings from that night. I came home from a friend's house and there it was…an unfinished letter. The feeling I had when I saw it still overtakes my body when I'm brought back to that night. A yellow piece of paper was laying on the entry step to my kitchen. Words covered the yellow piece of paper, words written in my husband's handwriting.

"Oh please God." I whispered as I covered my mouth trying to hold back the panicked scream that would surely wake my sleeping babies.

I could barely focus my eyes as I bent down to pick up that of page with a trembling hand. My mind was panicking, literally panicking with thoughts of: '*Did this happen, the thing we don't really like to talk about but, is always in the back of my mind?*' As I read the first sentence my trembling hand dropped the yellow piece of paper.

"My beloved, I love you so much but I just can't…" was written in my heroic, suffering husband's handwriting.

"Please no, God, please no." I whispered as I held my hand to my mouth so tightly that I could feel the pain of my teeth embedding into my upper lip; the pain seemed to keep my brain from panicking as I walked through the hallway to our room. *Holy cow, this was really happening.* The pure panic of the time had come. I had to face this. In my mind, I pictured the most horrific sights. *Why did my brain do that?* My two boys were in the house sleeping. I had to face this. I had to be strong. For my family.

I walked from our kitchen to a narrow hallway that literally seemed to be closing in on me. I glanced at my boys' bedroom doors to make sure they were closed. I don't even remember breathing. My heart was pounding right out of my neck. I slowly opened the door and I remember thinking, *my fear is coming true,* as I turned the almost heavy doorknob.

Three horrific scenarios played graphically through my mind.

After I opened the door, I pictured this six foot five man hanging from my bedroom ceiling. I looked up first. It's not that.

I thought about what it would look like when someone blew his head off. Jesse had kind of explained it to me. I looked at the bed. Okay. He was in the bed. I didn't see blood...a good sign. I still don't remember breathing.

Oh no, what if he took pills? I crawled into my ginormous, king-sized bed and hovered over him. I don't know how I even had the strength to do it because my whole body shook; trembled with shock. I just stared at him to see if his chest was rising and falling with each breath. I squinted so hard that it was almost like my eyes couldn't focus to see if he was breathing. I couldn't see the sheets move. My eyes hurt. I finally put my hand up to his face and slipped my trembling fingers under his nose.

PRAISE GOD! I felt his breath gently blow across my hand. It was such a soft, calm breath. I sighed with unimaginable relief as my shoulders dropped from their tense hold. I wanted to slap him awake and say *'Do you know what you just put me through?'* but wives of Veteran's with PTSD have to stay strong because, if we let them know that we're suffering, the chances of them hurting themselves are even stronger. We have to sacrifice for the better of our husbands. I let him sleep. I praised God that he was sleeping. Why? He hadn't slept in so many days. You see, it was nearing Memorial Day...

I let him sleep.

I finished the letter. He wrote about his best friend who was shot through the neck as Jesse tried to carry him to safety. He also wrote of how he was done with talking about his memories. He was over it. That is something we continue to work through, we now understand. My prayer is someday he accepts that PTSD will always be a part of our family; it's like the elephant in the room, sometimes a big, loud elephant.

He was over it.

Hupomone, patience, endurance, steadfastness; the ability to remain hopeful in times of waiting. Patient endurance. Can you see it? The patient endurance in your life, the confidence that God is doing something good? My goal is to show my PTSD suffering husband Christ's love through grace. Beautiful grace. God has equipped me for this story of my family, even if I have to explain to my boys why their daddy has "bad Army days." Would you take a few minutes and reflect on your life? What or who has God chosen you for? Are you in the midst of barely having a foothold on what seems to be a gigantic mountain?

Makrothumia, patience, forbearance, long-suffering; the ability to tolerate the fault and failures of others. Wow, right? Now that sounds like grace, don't you think? Romans 5:3-4 tells us to glory in our sufferings because we know that suffering produces perseverance; perseverance character; and character, hope. Not going to lie, every time I read that verse I get chills up my spine and an uncontrolled sigh comes out of me. Hope. It's what keeps us alive, keeps us moving forward, and keeps us climbing up that mountain. Hope is that little voice you hear that says, "You've got this, you can do this, you're almost there." I believe that hope allows us to see our situation through a whole new set of eyes. Through my journey I've always kept my eyes on the Lord, which gives me hope for a tomorrow that will blow my socks off, but I know that I need to have the perseverance to battle through this.

Courage is contagious. So will you be courageous with me? We can battle through life together, embracing vulnerability. Embracing vulnerability will allow us to experience joy. Amazing joy. Who is it that you won't quit on? I decided

Courage is contagious

not to quit on my husband. Ever. We will suffer together, celebrate together, trust God together, remain hopeful together, battle through this thing called PTSD together, and definitely laugh together. It is said that laughter reduces pain and allows us to tolerate discomfort. I've experienced the benefits of laughter from having a ridiculously funny husband. God designed him that way for a reason. A reason that is so clear to me now. And he created me to laugh with him...*God chose me.*

Mariska Hargitay:

"Surviving and thriving in the wake of...loss, I learned to believe in God. He has a plan, if you pay attention to the signs. I am inspired by the absolute proof of miracles."

REBECCA
GRAMBORT

Rebecca Grambort is a speaker, coach, and author. She is the founder of a Christian coaching business designed for women called Metamorphosis and His Masterpiece, LLC. She also is the founder of its networking group, "The Sisterhood" where she invites women to join her on a quest to live an extraordinary life. It is her passion to inspire, empower, and equip women for that very quest. Becca is also a distance runner and enjoys challenging herself by training for long distance races. She is a wife and a mother to four, and also enjoys downhill skiing and kayaking. Visit www.mahmonline.com for more information.

——— Chapter 6 ———

FROM MILLSTONE TO MEDAL

Rebecca Grambort

". . . and let us run with perseverance the race marked out for us . . ."

Hebrews 12:1 (NLT)

It was like the sound of a gun being fired off at the beginning of a race ... 3, 2, 1... BOOM! There was no rush of pounding feet to be heard slamming violently on the pavement. There was just the deafening sound of the violent pounding that was slamming in the void of my aching heart. Oh, I wanted to run; run away from my new reality. I wasn't trained for this kind of race. Heaven knows, I didn't even sign up for it! I felt like I was dying...yet *I* would get to live.

It was sunny and crisp weather the week after labor-day in 2007. My daughters and I had just moved into a beautiful home in the quaint village of Eagle, Wisconsin. It was the perfect area to start over and build a new life with what remained of my family. I sensed some relief from the burden I was carrying lift from around my neck. It had been a tough year, and I could breathe easier now knowing that we were safely home. **'Sanctuary' was the word to describe it, and that's exactly what I needed right now in the midst of my personal hell.**

My young daughters had just started back at their first day of school in our new community, and so I ventured out for my first run on the adjacent road near our new subdivision. How I desperately needed this time alone to process and pray.

Eagle was such a beautiful, inviting area, and I immediately felt nuzzled in its charm. As I ran, I took notice of a large majestic oak tree standing mightily alone in a field. It spoke to me silently about God's strength and majesty.

The smell of home flooded my senses, taking me away into a dream-like state. It was an escape from the reality of the new hell I needed to face. *'How can such unrelenting pain co-exist with such beauty?'* I was awestruck with the mystery of it. Other than my feet hitting the pavement, there had a profound quietness in that moment. A secure anchor below my raging storm was fastened deep inside of me. I quickly acknowledged my deep gratitude for it. Hellacious emotions of pain, confusion, and turmoil raged above, tossing me around like a ratty old rag doll.

It dawned on me in that moment that I had never been much of a runner. It certainly wouldn't have been a term I would have used to describe myself. I simply despised it. I realized that today, something had changed. My spirit shifted to a new place of thankfulness, and I recognized that it was a gift. I felt like I was able to run away from my new reality and run to the Heavens for help.

> *My spirit shifted to a new place of thankfulness.*

A shot of pain came searing through my heart, and I cried out to God: "Where did you put him? He's not anywhere!"

I couldn't see him in my dreams and the scent of his cologne had left the collar of his dress coat. He really was fading. "This hurts God! His little girls hurt. Please, help me." I pleaded and sobbed as I ran.

SILENCE.

Suddenly, I was struck by the deafening absence of sound and my body came crashing to a halt. If God was speaking, I couldn't hear him. As I stood there masking my face with my hands, weeping uncontrollably, I suddenly had a vision. It was a memory of myself in the hospital waiting room that bitter February. My husband had a routine surgery that had gone very awry. I was paging through the bible for comfort when I would receive a word from God I didn't understand, but at least it was something. A scripture was highlighted in a bright, white light:

"*Consider it pure joy, when you face trials of many kinds, because you know that the testing of your faith develops perseverance.*" (James 1:2-3 NIV)

My head spun in wonder. '*Is this a test?*' I thought, if I was faithful, I would receive the miracle I had been praying for: that my husband would live. I didn't receive that miracle. The news was inescapable. May 1, 2007, the doctors would tell me it was time to say goodbye to my husband and I held him as he took his final breaths.

I was crushed. *'How would I tell my girls?'* That would be the hardest news I would ever have to deliver. My senses returned to my new reality as I stood there weeping with my head in my hands. I was back on that silent run. I would have been grateful to hear anything. *'Anything God. Just please don't be silent.'* There was enough of that without Tom around. In a vision, I saw a millstone hanging from my neck. I hung my head, turned around, and slowly headed for home.

Looking back, little did I know that God was speaking a word of perseverance over my life through that scripture I'd seen when I'd been praying for my husband to live. I couldn't even begin to speculate what kind of perseverance would be required to survive the death of my spouse. I adored being a wife and a mother. When Tom died, I felt like half of who I was had been stripped away violently from me. I loved being a mom, but the joy of it had been suddenly sucked away. Those girls were my world. But so was he. And my identity was compromised.

Besides prayer, running would become one of the only healthy escapes I had during that dark season in my life. Day after day, I would run away from my new reality and run to the Heavens for help. If it weren't for my young daughters, I might have taken the ugly way out. I certainly wasn't prepared for the intensity of this race, and the battle between my spirit and flesh would begin to wage war inside of me. I caved in to drinking and began dating an old high school crush. This man was a shot of Novocain to my aching heart. I lacked the patience and perseverance it would take to stay grounded, and I turned to him instead. That invisible millstone that hung around my neck would increase in size and in weight time and time again.

A year later, I would find myself pregnant and in a painful rebound marriage. Life would begin to spiral out of control for me and, because of my lack of patience, I would begin to complicate an already messy situation. My new marriage quickly fell apart and a divorce was inevitably on the horizon. My soon to be ex-husband's sectional sleeper sofa couldn't leave soon enough. I got sick of waiting for him to remove it and so I hauled it out of the house myself! What a mistake. I severely injured my back and that would cost me one of my only coping skills – running.

Over those next few years, I would need to learn to persevere through extreme emotional *and* physical pain. I had put myself in a good hard corner.

*I was in a financial pit from spending excessive money on
this man and his children.

*I was a mother of an infant with no help from that same man.
*I would need to dig myself out of a financial pit by cleaning
homes, waitressing and catering all while in terrific pain.

My heart broke for my children. They were all now fatherless, and my heart ached when young Ty would pray at night for a Dad that would stay. I had to cling to the faithfulness and love of the

Heavenly Father who promised that He would never leave us. I put my trust in Him to Father my now fatherless children.

I continued "running" to the Heaven's for help, and God would send His angelic protection time and time again. Those angels didn't ease my emotional pain, but in those moments I realized that I wasn't alone. They gathered and counted my every tear. The more desperate I was for Jesus, the more intimately acquainted I became with Him.

It was through that wilderness season in my life that I experienced His Goodness. He revealed His character to me time and time again as I learned to trust Him as provider, protector and comforter. He was so good to me, and the suffering strangely became sweet. With His guide, I would find a home church to get rooted deeper in my faith and in my Christian community. There I would be met by a woman who would breathe hope into my dying situation. *'Not only so, but we rejoice in our sufferings, because we know that suffering produces perseverance.'* (Romans 5:3 NIV)

Tears came flooding down my face as I recalled the scripture from James that came leaping off those pages that February of 2007. She was speaking the same words aloud to me from a different part of the Bible. I suddenly pieced together that God was asking me to persevere from the very beginning. Time went on, and Kim, the woman who had brought me hope again, would quickly become my mentor and friend. She had the skills that I was lacking and she taught me what to do.

Make a decision to not make an emotional decision.

"Make a decision not to make an emotional decision." She wisely advised.

This would be the first life skill I would struggle to learn. Let me tell you, it took more strength to control myself and "do nothing" and not react to my reality than it did to haul that sectional sleeper sofa out of my house! It was the hardest thing I had ever done, yet it gained the greatest reward.

When I was in Kim's presence, I could feel that invisible millstone miraculously lift. She infused me with hope and challenged me to see myself the way that God saw me. *'Was I something more than just a wife or mother?'* A seed had been planted, and I felt the movement of new life stir inside of it. I started feeding my brain with the word of God, and I began to practice giving thanks. I counted all of my blessings, each and every day: 1, 2, 3 ... starting with the heads of each of my children.

Over those next few years, perseverance and praise would become a way of life for me, and I would begin to take my eyes off of my own pain and begin to help other single moms in need. My identity was no longer found in just the role of wife or mom and I discovered who I really was. It was an identity that could not be stripped away. With or without a husband, I had a purpose. I had survived going through hell, and for the first time, I began to find peace, "alone".

Six long years had passed and it was once again labor-day week. The year was now 2013. The windows in my home were cracked open and I took note of the familiar sunny and crisp weather that followed me over those seasons. I was just arising in bed that morning when something unique happened. My home was still serving as a sanctuary to me, and I felt gratitude rise in my heart.

The returning of the new school year caused me to reflect and I thought of how much time had passed. I had been through a lot: from the death of my spouse, to an unexpected son, to the death of a marriage and the pain that took up residency in my body. It had been a bittersweet journey and a myriad of memories of God's faithfulness darted around in my head. My thoughts were interrupted by the pitter-patter of little feet. It was my son venturing from his room to find me.

As I embraced my energetic little boy and kissed him on the cheek, I immediately felt freedom race through my body. Something had changed. There was absence of the pain that had made its home in my leg. I brushed it off as a temporary window of relief and I gave Ty a lingering, heartfelt hug. I was torn between sending him off to K-4 for the first time and keeping him all to myself. I was going to miss him so much. Yet, I also had a sense of relief as I realized the desperate break that I needed as a single mom.

After dropping my children off at school, I was reminded of the sudden tranquility running through my body. There was no sharp pain running down my leg. Because of this, I would decide to venture out for a walk on that familiar road near our home. I stopped to gaze at the majestic oak tree that still stood mightily alone in that field. It spoke to me silently about God's strength and majesty. The smell of home flooded my senses once again taking me away into a dream-like state. I remembered and acknowledged that secure anchor fastened deep inside of me. I was deeply grateful for it and suddenly recognized that it had been there all along. I just couldn't realize it over the clambering of my raging storm. My leg didn't hurt, and I noticed that, due to habit, I was still walking with a shorter stride favoring that leg. *'It couldn't be gone. I had stopped praying for that miracle years ago.'* I reasoned. SILENCE. If God was speaking, I couldn't hear Him. *'Maybe God gracefully honored my praise to Him over those painful seasons in my life.'* I thought to myself. More silence surrounded me. All I knew was that it was to His Glory. I was awestruck and grateful for it.

"Thank You, Lord," I repeated, as tears of gratitude streamed down my face. A few hours passed as I walked away and thanked the Heavens for help. I had lost track of the time, and I needed to get back for Ty. I smiled, held my head high, and quickly headed for home.

Over that week, I quickly began to dream up what else I could do. *'Maybe if I can walk, I can run?'*, and I could! Three miles turned into four, and four turned into seven. Then on one of my runs on a brisk fall day, I heard the Lord indicate that more miracles were coming their way. *'This will be your heaping year.'* A scripture dropped into my spirit: "gift upon gift" (John 1:16 AMP) *'What else could possibly be coming?'* I thought as I ran, giddy with anticipation.

A short while later, I would meet a man who was widowed and shared my love for the Lord. We shared stories of miracles and loss, and how God used these events to draw us closer to Him. He proceeded to tell me about how his young daughter had received a new heart. What great loss both of our families had experienced, yet, what great miracles we both had witnessed. Both of us had lost our spouses and each of our children had lost a parent either to death or by abandonment. Our hearts grew quickly together and we had hopes to be married.

Then one bitter winter day I would see the manifestation of more miracles on their way. I was on my treadmill as I gazed out the window and "ran away" to the Heaven's for help. "Lord, I don't even know if it's okay to ask this. Forgive me if it's not. Lord, I would like Ty's father removed for this season of his life while he is still an unfit Father. You know it is the desire of Ty's heart and that he has been praying for a Dad that will stay. Lord, again forgive me if it is wrong to pray this. But your word does say "A man reaps what he sows...and he has sown nothing, let him reap nothing!" Suddenly, I saw an enormous white cloud appear in the crisp blue sky. Jesus was standing there on it in white with his arms stretched out. Countless angels in white surrounded him. It seemed the angels were sent on assignment and they swooped away. I gasped and brought myself to a halt. *"The T.P.R. angels!"*, I audibly shouted. Astonishment flooded my mind. The angels were going to assist in the Termination of Parental Rights! I thought, as I trembled with excitement and fear.

"Oh Lord, leave some warring angels here. This might be a battle!" And it was. It wasn't much more than a week or two later I would receive the news that Ty's father was willing to terminate his parental rights. More miracles certainly were on their way. Gift upon gift. It was in that moment that I would feel an urgency increase to be married. How would I tell my son? That would be the second hardest news I would ever have to deliver. Except this time with a miracle of His answered prayer. Ty would receive the gift of a Dad "that would stay." And I would get to witness the adoption of Father mentioned in scripture carried out in the natural.

That spring I would be married and relocate my family over the summer to Northern Wisconsin. I was heartbroken to leave the home that was like a sanctuary to me, but there was little reason to hold onto it. Brian had terminated his rights and my new husband had officially adopted my son at the age of five. I knew that road ahead and blending our families wouldn't be easy, yet I was confident that our faith was strong enough to see us through.

Relocating and blending a family would pose many new unforeseen challenges. Persevering would require even more grit. I would find the escape that running continued to provide for me as I ventured out on the back roads of my new home, and continue to run to the Heavens for help. Seven miles turned into nine and nine turned into thirteen. I felt my drive shift into a new gear for the mountain ahead. Running would strengthen me for my new duties at home as a new wife to a man I was still getting to know. All of us would need time to bond. All of the different personality types between us and new power struggles posed a myriad of unsavory challenges. It caused a great strain on all of us, and me and my kids struggled to find our way in our new home and community. There were many times I wanted to give up.

I ran and I prayed, "I can't do this without you, Lord. But, I am thankful that I can. Thank you for this gift."

May of 2015 had arrived … 3, 2, 1 … BOOM!

The rush of feet slamming on the pavement invaded my surroundings. I was running my very first race, a half marathon. I felt like nothing could stop me after I finished that race. A beautiful finisher's medal graced my neck as I held my head high.

The millstone had been replaced.

Running was helping me to envision, with the help of my mentor, who I was becoming and who I was created to be. I wanted to inspire and lead women in my new area. Like I needed my mentor, I sensed that someone out there needed me too. I was determined to keep my eyes focused on my purpose and not on my pain. I was becoming a distance runner not only in the natural, but in the spirit, to run the best race of my life.

God began speaking to me on those runs and He would give me visions as He helped me design a Christian organization for women. As I trained for my race, I trained for the call on my life and I became an inspirational speaker, coach, and author. I would begin leading in my new area all while I trained for and ran my very first full marathon in September of 2016. Over that year, I would beat my personal goals as a distance runner and I would place in my age division, taking third. I even surprised myself with a first place divisional medal the following year! Running, blending a family, and leading women in my new area stretched me in a new way I could have never imagined. The weightiness of blending a family especially would make it feel as if I had that old millstone tied around my neck at times. But as I reviewed and counted my victories in my life, I could see that those feelings of defeat were merely no more than just lies from the pit of hell.

This summer, I would have an opportunity to take a sixteen-mile training run back near my old home. My daughters were adults now and were making their way back in our old community. I felt torn between my two homes, especially now that my girls had moved away. I was about seven miles in when I discovered that if I looped through Eagle, I could run past our old house and onto that familiar road adjacent to our home. When I approached my old home, I felt a violent slamming return to my heart. I felt like an unwelcomed spy and hoped that none of my neighbors would spot me. How I desperately longed to walk through that house, hoping it would take away the feeling that it still somehow belonged to me. A piece of my heart still lived there. I quickly rushed along and onto the adjacent road.

I gasped with emotion as I stopped to gaze at the large majestic oak tree that still stood mightily alone in that field. It still spoke to me about God's strength and majesty. That old violent slamming of pain was pounding on my aching heart once again, and I came crashing to a halt. "This is where our journey together began Lord.", I audibly prayed. I could feel His great and silent Love for me in spite of the searing pain in my heart. I longed for my old home. "I can't look back. It is not wise. I must look ahead." "Wherever you are, is where my home is, and You are everywhere I go." SILENCE. If God was speaking, I couldn't hear Him. But in that moment, my spirit had a great revelation. Although I never identified myself as a runner years ago, I suddenly realized that I always had been one. My God who had performed a healing miracle in my back, had passed the baton onto me. In those moments, I would be given the choice to persevere and create my own miracles because of it. He gave me the power to turn my millstone into a medal. With His help, I would go from millstone to medal; millstone to miracle, time and time again. My heart leapt with gratitude as I leapt forward to head for "home".

Saint Augustine:

"Faith is to believe what you do not see; the reward of this faith is to see what you believe."

JANET

BYRNE

Janet Byrne is a public speaker and writer who resides in Waukesha, Wisconsin with her husband, Yancy, and two sons, Grant and Gavin. Whether singing on the church worship team or speaking to women of all ages and walks of life, Janet's passion to share the love of God is the bedrock of who she is. Her greatest desire is to see women grasp who God is and who they are in Him: wonderfully made, deeply loved, and highly favored! You can follow Janet at: www.janetbyrne.org.

———— Chapter 7 ————

CHASING BUTTERFLIES

Janet Byrne

"So do not fear, for I am with you; do not be dismayed, for I am your God. I will strengthen you and help you; I will uphold you with my righteous right hand."

∽ *Isaiah 41:10 (NIV)*

Years ago I attended a weekly bible study. It met on Wednesday nights and was often the highlight of my week. We began each study as a large group worshipping, and anyone who knows me knows I love to worship. You could hear me singing down the hall and around the corner, arms raised high; I sang my heart out in praise. Then we broke down into smaller groups. I was one of the small group leaders who facilitated the conversation among us. This came easy for me as I love to talk! No wonder I went to college and graduated with a Communications Degree. I have always loved being around people and talking with them. So much so that when I was a young girl and would visit my grandma, she would often play the "How long can you be quiet game?" I was quite the chatter box. On this particular night, I remember being in a spunky mood. I skipped into the small group and sat beside and across from my Jesus loving friends. I shared that I wanted to do something really BIG for God. I think I had just seen a story on the news of a young boy collecting shoes for kids overseas and I thought, *why him...why not me?* I wasn't sure what I wanted to do exactly, I just knew I wanted it to be BIG! The bigger the better! Hats for newborns; coats for the homeless; a mission trip; there must be something I could do. We all laughed and went about the rest of our study. Little did I know at that time just how BIG my life story would become and the something BIG that was in store for me.

Months passed and that spunky small group leader lost her spunk. Two previous diagnoses had caught up to me. The first being Rheumatoid Arthritis. RA is inflammation in the muscles and joints. The second was Polymyositis. Polymyositis is inflammation that decides to attack an internal organ, which, in my case, was my lungs. Up until this point, I was able to live a pretty normal life...with disease. I was busy getting married, having babies, speaking, and serving on different committees;

however, the scar tissue in my lungs had also been busy. It was now limiting my ability to breathe and perform daily tasks. I began parking as close to the door as possible, taking the elevator instead of the stairs and unfortunately walking down that long hallway to the large group left me so winded that singing loudly turned into coughing and wheezing loudly instead. My greatest desire was no longer wanting to do something BIG for God but rather wanting God to do something BIG for me... I needed a miracle!

I have never been one to like doctor's appointments. I imagine I'm not alone. I have also never been one to like surprises and for me the two go hand in hand. Going to an appointment always turned into a surprise of some sort. Something typically happened that I wasn't expecting and I'd usually leave upset. So I did everything I could to avoid doctors. However, my body was telling me it needed one...or many.

I had been working part-time where I sat at my desk more and walked around less. I took naps on my lunch break at home. Then after work, I would plop myself down on the couch and crash, jacket still on. Putting on pajamas never happened. I showered once every other day instead of every day. I was tired; so tired! I had started running a fever during this time, too. So, I knew my body was sick. I was fighting a virus or something and I just couldn't sleep enough. I no longer had the strength and stamina to go to work. I ended up taking some vacation days as my appointment with a new doctor was right around the corner. It was at this time that I switched pulmonologists.

As my husband and I walked into the doctor's office, my heart raced with the anticipation of what this new doctor might say.

How would the appointment go?

What would he hear when he listened to my lungs?

Would he be able to see how sick I had become just by looking at me?

We started with a weight check. I came in at a whopping one hundred thirteen pounds. "What?" I was shocked. I knew I had lost a little weight, but not that much. The nurse then asked me to do a six-minute walk. I looked at her and with tears in my eyes said "I can't do it. Please don't make me walk for six minutes." At that moment six minutes felt like six hours and I just couldn't do it.

She then proceeded to put a pulse oximeter on my finger and within seconds, the beeping began. I could tell she was now nervous too as she said, "Oh sweetheart, you're not oxygenating very well. You are only at seventy eight percent." The doctor came into the examining room. He took one look at me; one look at the seventy eight percent, and within minutes I was hooked up to an oxygen tank. All the while crying, I was told that I was one sick girl and my lungs were in very rough shape.

We discussed the pneumonia I had come down with, the scarring in my lungs and the progression of the disease; how irreversible the damage was…and we discussed the possibility of a transplant. I sat up on the examining table, the white paper shuffling under me as I fidgeted and listened to these facts. I wanted so badly to pretend this wasn't my life. The concerned look on the doctor's face spoke volumes and scared me.

He was soft spoken as he shared my two options: I could be admitted and monitored closely for the next two weeks. During time I would receive IV antibiotics ...or... I could go home and come back daily. I, of course, chose the second option. I had never been fond of hospitals. When I was a little girl, around six years old, I saw my grandpa in the hospital, lots of tubes and machines. The sights and sounds freaked me out!

We drove home with a steady flow of tears streaming down my cheeks. The sounds of sniffling and oxygen puffing were deafening. I had never been more scared. I had never felt so ugly. I had tubes coming out of my nose, attached to a tank that I couldn't get rid of, hide, or pretend wasn't there. Here I sat, next to my hunk of a husband. He's a six foot, burly, blond, and loves everything "active". And here he was stuck with a wife on oxygen; a total mess!

Of course, that wasn't how he felt, but it was definitely how I did. I saw a face in the mirror that day that I didn't recognize. Big black bags under my eyes, cheeks sunken in, and I started to believe the lies it would tell me. You are ugly. You are sick. You are not worthy of healing. You are not going to get better. God doesn't love you. You are going to die. I remember telling my husband how ugly I felt and that I didn't want to leave the house. He told me I was beautiful and this was temporary. OUR plan was to ditch the oxygen after the infection had cleared up.

I had two small boys waiting for me at grandma and grandpa's house, and had NO idea what I was going to tell them. Only six and four at the time, how would I explain the oxygen? How could I possibly hold it together for them when my world had just come crashing down on me and I was falling apart. If we could have just stayed in the car and drove for hours I would have been content. I kept saying, "I am just not ready...not ready to see everyone." We pulled into my parent's driveway, I stayed in the car. I could see the fear in the boy's eyes and could sense it as they ran to Daddy. I understood, I was just as scared as they were, but needed to put on a brave face. All the while crumbling inside. "Mommy is sick boys and needs this to help her breathe," I hesitantly told them.

I spent the next two weeks driving back and forth to the doctor's office; an hour each way for IV antibiotics. Kicking the pneumonia was our top priority. At every appointment, my nurse Tina, always upbeat, would give me a pep talk. She was my angel during this time. Speaking life over my body. She shared stories of a man who had a transplant and was doing well, and this gave me hope!

The infection began to clear, but my lung function remained the same. About two weeks after that initial appointment, I was rushed to the ER with an extremely high pulse and blood pressure. I had developed blood clots in my lungs and was now in the place I had feared most...the hospital.

FEAR...I've spent the majority of my life battling it. When I was six, my best friend died. She died and I was faced with seeing my grandpa in the hospital within days of each other! Although Angela died physically, I died mentally. My happy go lucky self died. My "life is all about rainbows and unicorns" died and I became crippled by the fear of sickness and death.

For years I pleaded with God not to let me get sick and die.

For years I pleaded with God to not let me get sick and die. My thought was if it could happen to Angela, why couldn't it happen to me! I shared a bedroom with my sister and would often lay awake at night in fear that she would possibly get sick. I still hate the stomach flu! So here I was on oxygen, told I needed a life saving transplant, and had developed pulmonary embolisms. It was more than I could handle and I began having regular panic attacks.

I remember one Sunday, my husband Yancy wanted to take the boys and me to a park to have a picnic and feed the ducks. As we drove further and further away from home my heart began to race more and more. Yancy kept asking me if I wanted him to turn around and although everything in me wanted to say yes, I didn't want to disappoint the boys. I just wanted so badly to feel the love and presence of God; to feel peace. I thought if He really truly loved me, this wouldn't be happening. I had become a beggar "God can you please, will you just, I need to know if you really…" When we got to the park, I was paralyzed with fear and couldn't get out of the car. I watched the boys feed the ducks from a distance and called my girlfriend sobbing. So thankful for the friends God gave me during this time! She prayed with me and helped calm me down!

I spent about two weeks going through testing to be listed. The outpatient tests took place a few days each week over a two-week period. Growing up, I'd been surrounded by a lot of fear filled kind of thinking, and I struggled to renew my mind to think positively. I was going through so much fear and I really felt like I was going to die. I didn't have a lot of hope and the experience exasperated my negativity…my dread.

I.

Was.

Going.

To.

Die.

Would I be a good candidate for a transplant?
Would they find something wrong with me?
Would I be able to be listed?

The tests went on and on from head to toe: CT scans, a bone density scan, mammogram, colonoscopy, endoscopy, every imaginable cancer test (if it was detected, I wouldn't be listed). I had to do pulmonary function tests to measure my breathing. I would take a six-minute walk and doctors would measure how far I could go and what happened to my blood oxygenation.

Then, there was the heart catheterization. I thought they were going to go through my groin and I'd be sedated; instead, they went through my carotid artery and I received no sedation. I had to lay completely still for what felt like forever, but was more like 45 minutes. They went through my neck to get to my heart. Making this even worse was that they decided to draw blood from this gaping neck hole because they had such a huge vein. Thirty viles of blood were pulled from me and tested for countless different things.

Something was going to be wrong.

I wasn't going to get listed.

I pictured my kids without a mom.

I pictured my husband without a wife.

The fearful thoughts continued to flood my brain.

During the heart catheterization, as I laid on the gurney without any sedation, the nurse commented on my toes . . .

My girlfriend had just taken me for a pedicure and I had flowers painted on them. If only I had felt as pretty as my pink painted toes! The results came back and the doctor said, "Your heart looks good." But in that moment my heart was anything but good. I wanted to scream, "My heart isn't good. It's broken, it's been ripped apart and I'm questioning everything." *Where is God right now? Is He really a good God? Does He really love me? Answer prayers? Heal the sick? Is He punishing me for my past sins?* All of the things that I had thought I knew about God were now open for debate. My heart was a mess!

In early June, I was officially listed for transplant.

I realized in these moments that although I had professed to know God, I really didn't believe what His word said. It became much easier for me to believe Satan's lies than God's truth and I felt like a little girl holding a dandelion playing the He loves me, He loves me not game. I spent much of that summer in tears; wrestling with God. Instead of enjoying our family time together, I was picturing their lives without me.

Yancy had lost his brother, grandmother and brother–in–law all within the year. So of course I kept thinking I was next; that somehow God was preparing him for my passing as he processed the loss of his other family members. Because of course that was the view I now had of God. We prayed together at night, and I found myself begging once again for healing. Crying out on my knees asking God what I needed to do to be seen as pleasing in His sight. Thinking that maybe just maybe if he was pleased with me, then He would heal this body. I had known the verse "the prayer of the righteous avail much" so I decided I must not be righteous or my prayers would be answered. I couldn't figure out what I needed to do more; more prayers, more quiet times, more confessing, repenting, Bible reading, loving, forgiving…what was the more that I needed to do?

It felt like my identity was being stripped away. All of the things that I had loved doing… dinner with friends, shopping at the mall, playing with the boys, SINGING, even as much as making

CHASING BUTTERFLIES ————

lunches or doing laundry, I was no longer able to do. On a good day I was able to take a shower but that was maybe once a week.

God has always used music to speak to me…and birds. He used an owl to tell me that I was supposed to marry Yancy and a hawk to tell me my pregnancy with Gavin would go okay. Gavin's name means white hawk. So, I shouldn't have been surprised when I got a card in the mail one day telling me about the butterfly.

It came from a dear friend from that weekly bible study. She had drawn the wings of butterflies on the paper and shared how they resembled the lobes of our lungs. She continued to explain how my life and situation mimicked the life of a butterfly. That I was that caterpillar bound up in a cocoon but that just like a butterfly, I would break out, spread my new wings (lungs) and fly. From that day on, butterflies had taken on a new meaning for me. I would see them and sensed they were a touch; a hug from God. They told me I would make it to transplant. My new wings (lungs) were coming. I began seeing butterflies all around me and at just the right times.

One day as I was crying, I will never forget going to the bathroom to wipe my tears and realized the toilet paper I reached for had butterflies on it. I just sat there, on the toilet, crying, laughing, and then crying some more as I felt the hug from God in that moment. "You're gonna be okay," He told me. My miracle was coming.

Another time, I showed up at a family event, extremely weepy, only to have a conversation with a relative who had butterfly earrings on. You couldn't miss them. She had NO idea that I had gotten this note in the mail or that her earrings would be a hug from Heaven that I desperately needed in that moment.

104

Butterflies on houses, necklaces, sweaters, cars and in places ONLY GOD could put them, at just the right time... just for ME!

God was using butterflies to tell me how much He DID love me, that He had never left me and that He was actually carrying me. I began reading my Bible more and more, and the verses I had read a million times before were now taking on new meaning. I learned there was "no condemnation for those who are in Jesus "and that meant me. I could stop beating myself us for past sins and instead accept His amazing love, mercy and grace. I met a sweet gal during this time, I call her KLOVE Lisa, and she opened my eyes to TRUTH and God's will regarding healing. Faith began rising up in me as we prayed together and began claiming His promises over my body!

Winter came and my dear friend, Jill, contacted me, and asked if I would share my story at her church's Christmas tea that year. She had been reading my email updates and knew how God was using butterflies to encourage my spirit. Wheezing and winded, I stood up and shared how God was loving on me during my trials and how I was being changed.

A few days later, Jill contacted me and said, "Janet, I have something for you." There was a woman in the crowd that morning that had been to Israel months earlier. She had gone to the marketplace and was drawn to a particular scarf. She said she kept walking away from it but God kept bringing her back to it. She didn't know why as she knew it wasn't for her. You would understand if you saw the scarf. But out of obedience she bought it, brought it home, and tucked it in her closet. As she listening to my story that winter morning she instantly had her answer. Here I was talking about my precious butterflies and here she sat with a HUGE scarf in her closet that had HUGE orange and black butterflies on it. Yes, orange and black, and yes HUGE! I have never seen anything like it. God, in His Awesomeness, reached down from Heaven and gave me a Christmas gift that I could have never dreamt up or imagined if I tried!

> *God, in His Awesomeness, reached down from Heaven and gave me a Christmas gift.*

To this day, I have such a precious reminder, a scarf, of HIS precious love for me!

In August 2011, the call came. It was time for me to break free from my cocoon. I was more than ready. I had been transformed spiritually and mentally and was now ready for my transformation physically. I had learned what it meant to trust God. That His word is true and I could stand on it regardless of what my eyes could see. I had learned that He loves me, He loves me, He LOVES me. There was no He loves me not! And although I sure loved my butterflies, I no longer found myself chasing after them.

As we drove to the hospital, I was filled with excitement...and peace!

At the hospital, I was quickly surrounded by family and friends. We spent the night praying, wondering, waiting... we certainly didn't sleep much. The next morning as I was wheeled down for surgery, I was on a gurney, in front of an elevator, saying goodbye to my husband as that was the "see you soon" spot. He prayed with me, kissed my forehead and the elevator doors opened. What I saw next was nothing shy of a miracle.

The ceiling of the elevator was lit up with a scene of a sky and BUTTERFLIES!

And a song that I had listened to countless times before was instantly brought to my mind... by The Afters:

When I'm feeling all alone
With so far to go
The signs are nowhere on this road
Guiding me home
When the night is closing in
It's falling on my skin
Oh God, will you come close?

You light, light, light up the sky
You light up the sky to show me
You are with me

And I can't deny
No I can't deny that You are right here with me
You've opened my eyes
So I can see you all around me

You light, light, light up the sky
Light up the sky to show me
You are with me

So I run straight into Your arms
You're the bright and morning Sun
To show your love
There's nothing You Won't do

I had a double lung transplant that day. But more importantly, over the course of the year I had had a heart, mind, soul and spirit transplant as well! I had been changed from the inside out in more ways that I can share. My desire to do something BIG for God was realized as I stepped out in faith. I am convinced that when we have a BIG faith, we are doing something BIG for Him. It may not have been shoes, hats or a mission trip but it was MY BIG something and I get spunky just thinking about it! Who would have thought…a double lung transplant?!

I still see butterflies all the time and am constantly reminded of my metamorphosis, my new lungs, and my miracle!

Joel Osteen:

"I believe if you keep your faith, you keep your trust, you keep the right attitude, if you're grateful, you'll see God open up new doors."

LUANNE
NELSON

A professional photographer, *Luanne Nelson* has a keen eye for balance, design and symmetry. Her photos have been showcased in several fine art galleries in Alaska and Wisconsin. She studied English Literature at Westminster College in Pennsylvania and Journalism at Marquette University in Wisconsin. Luanne and her husband David share a spirit of adventure and lived in Alaska for a few years. Some of their favorite places include British Columbia and St. Petersburg in Russia. Both ordained ministers, Luanne and David currently reside in Milwaukee, Wisconsin. Luanne's web site is: www.LuanneNelson.com.

—— Chapter 8 ——

GRATEFUL FOR HIS MERCY

Luanne Nelson

"But we are not those who turn back and are lost. No, we are the people who have faith and are saved."

Hebrews 10:39 (ERV)

I am old. It surprises me. It happened so fast. But here I am; old. Not as old as my grandmother when she went to heaven. Not as old as Sister Mary Josephine, who made the best oatmeal cookies in the world and shared them while they were warm with the little second graders down the hall from the convent kitchen. I can still remember sitting at my desk picking out the raisins to enjoy separately. Back in those days, I wore a teeny, navy blue jumper and a crisp white blouse, and shoes with shiny buckles. Today, I prefer to be shoeless and wear a lot of black. I think it looks good with my usually messy blonde-gray hair.

I've had an interesting life. I think we all have, really. I wouldn't want to live it all over again although I wouldn't mind being forty-nine again either. Maybe forty-nine for about three years and then pick up where I left off. I met the love of my life when I was forty-nine. I know, I know. It took me long enough. David and I are still married which is a miracle in itself. I am not good at marriage. Good thing he is.

Speaking of miracles, since this is a miracle book, I am going to share two of them that happened to me in my life so far. There have been many or I would be dead by now. In any event, here are two of my favorites.

The First Miracle: The Smoking Hot Nun

I loved smoking cigarettes. I loved everything about it – the fire, the smoke, the rush, the air-art of jagged mountains that would fade in a breeze. At first, I used it as a prop on the stage of college life – journalism to be exact. A cigarette in hand, I instantly became an imaginary reporter in a dark and smoky room with a single light bulb suspended over my typewriter as I reported breaking news produced on the incoming newswires click click click click. My ashtray overflowed, each cig-stub represented another seven minutes spent constructing the perfect story.

I loved smoking cigarettes.

I didn't graduate as a reporter, instead I traveled, married and reared a few children. I unraveled, married again (and again) and patched my life back together several times over. The blue smoke remained a constant. Cigs, you see, became my best friends. All twenty in a row – always there, always dependable, always pleasurable, always standing ready at attention like little white papered soldiers with tan boots in my flip-top box of life.

I smoked in Paris and felt trés chic. I smoked at the Vatican and felt like a racy little sinner. I became Audrey Hepburn with her sleek little black cig holder as long as her neck. I was a fashion model using cigs to keep my weight down, punctuating my puffs with a spoonful of yogurt here and there and an occasional snickers bar to keep me going.

This went on for years – and years – and years. **I evened out at two-packs-a-day and kept that going for what seemed like forever.** There was a streak of time when I thought I was smoking three packs a day – turns out, other models were raiding my stash. I was relieved. Two was okay; three a bit excessive. Two going at one time was weird, but that happened sometimes, too.

I knew I was damaging my lungs but since I couldn't see them it really didn't matter to me. I imagined my lungs were blackening but honestly I really didn't care. I could have swallowed a canary and it wouldn't have flown back out simply because I knew for a fact it would fly right past my lungs without so much as even noticing them. Then, they would get all tangled up in peristaltic action never to fly back up and out anyway. The canary test didn't apply, so therefore I was still okay.

Besides, my skin was still a healthy pink without wrinkles except for a few around the corners of my mouth like what nuns get from pursing their lips from being in the perpetual state of too much disdain. I related to the disdainful nuns and lit up another one. I wondered if I could smoke if I entered a convent.

Strangely enough, it was my molars that started to protest my lifestyle. "Every time you inhale, you are strangling a tooth. That's why you need so many root canals. You are constricting your capillaries and not feeding the canals," said my dentist. I really did not want to hear this. I could live with imaginary blackened lungs and a wrecked heart, (heck, I lived through the heartbreak of a few lousy relationships, cigs were not going to do my heart in any more than it already had been done in.) But, my *teeth*? No one had warned me about that. All of a sudden, this was real and these root canals were getting expensive.

God has a marvelous sense of humor. I had fallen big time for the bearer of these bad tooth-tidings. Yes, I had the hots for my dentist. As a matter of fact, I was teeth over heels. I called him up and asked him out for coffee. My friends were going to duct tape my mouth shut to keep me from talking about him all the time. Anyway, I called him and he liked me alright and we were about to meet his Mother. The problem was this – his Mother lived almost four hours away by car.

Now, anyone who smokes knows the joy of smoking in the car on a road trip. Fine tunes blaring, the freedom of the open road with continual heavenly puffs of relaxation. Also, smoking helped to cut down on the snacking thus maintaining that svelte physique that had been in place for decades following that first puff ever (which, of course, was punctuated with severe coughing and the acute inability to breathe).

A road trip with my darling dentist with whom I was hopelessly in love meant – oh no – I could not smoke during the entire trip. Four hours of rolling over ribbons of pavement without so much as a hint of smoky fun. This was a serious dilemma.

So, I took it to my girlfriends during a smoking break at work. What to do what to do? How in the world am I going to pull this off? My little soldier-friends-in-a-box continued to stand at attention, expressionless, loyally remaining at my beck and call. One by one, my girlfriends snuffed out their smokes and went back into the building leaving me there alone to ponder (panic) alone.

It's really difficult to tell you what happened next. Not because it's sad, rather, because it's just unlike anything I've ever said out loud - and, as you can probably tell, I talk a lot. I'm going to try to tell you though, so please bear with me.

I stood out there and lit up another one. I inhaled deeply. When I looked up, I saw a nicely dressed gentleman standing about an arm and a half's length away from me. I was startled because I had been deep in thought and didn't see him approaching. I vividly recall he had very kind eyes which softened the startle. He smiled and said, "I overheard you say that you needed to stop smoking." I thought to myself, *what a nosy person – and an eavesdropper to boot!* He continued, "I went through that a few years ago and haven't smoked since."

Thankfully, I was standing right next to the door that opened into the building in the event I had to make a quick exit from this stranger who had just barged into my life without being welcomed. This door thought gave me comfort. Nonetheless, since I was curious, I politely asked him to tell me how he had been able to stop smoking. After all, that did seem to be the question of the day. He answered...

"Pray often. Pray a lot."

Alrighty. Confirmed. This well-dressed eavesdropper was indeed just a holy-roller nutcase. I thanked him for his thoughts, told him I prayed a lot already and began opening the door to the building. He added this as I opened the door...

"Ask God to smoke for you."

Flee! My inner sinner shouted. I quickly opened the door. The stranger continued talking and added, "God loves you and doesn't want you to be sick. Smoking won't make Him sick – let Him smoke for you. Every time you want a cigarette, ask Him to smoke it for you." There was a sense of commanding urgency in his voice.

This, of course, stopped me in my tracks. I really don't know how long I stood there, but when I looked up, he was gone. I searched the area with my eyes, and there was not a sign of him anywhere.

There is absolutely no way I could have thought this up on my own. It was way too weird. I had to admit that it did make sense, though. God could not get sick – He could take my addiction from me – relieve me – prevent me from getting sick – all I had to do was *Ask Him to smoke for me*. A strange feeling of protection, care and calmness – of love, really – swept over me as I opened the door and headed back to my work area.

I didn't say anything when I got back to my desk because the whole thing seemed just plain too big and too strange to tell anyone at work. I felt the need to sort and think and sort some more.

A few days later, on April 23rd, 2004 at 5:04 CDT (I looked at my car clock) traveling south on Oakland Avenue, I inhaled, exhaled and tossed my last cig out the window of my car. I looked in the rearview mirror and watched it bounce on the pavement.

Yes, I littered in the throes of a miracle.

It has been said that God chooses the biggest sinners and uses them to show His mercy and love. I have to agree, because I am far from holy and in the following days He must have smoked a few hundred cigarettes for me. The cravings became less and less as the days passed. It was totally amazing – I would think about having a cig (like every few minutes at first) and as soon as I asked Him to smoke it for me, the thought immediately was gone until the next time I wanted one. The times got further and further apart until I really didn't think about smoking at all anymore.

That was almost fourteen years ago. I truly do believe an angel visited me that day at work. Thank you, dear Lord Jesus.

And yes, I enjoyed a smoke-free road trip and did meet my darling dentist's Mother. Her son, David, and I have been married for over a dozen years now.

Hebrews 13:2 Forget not to show love unto strangers: for thereby some have entertained angels unaware.

The Second Miracle: Back to Jesus

Early in our marriage, David and I decided to relocate to Alaska. We had honeymooned there in the summertime, and it was both geographically spectacular and enchanting. Since we had married each other later in life, we figured the Land of the Midnight Sun would give us twice the life for the buck since it stayed light all day and night in the summertime. We could have two days in one! We hadn't considered the winter darkness and ended up driving home nearly six years later in June of 2013. There is more to it, but that's a different miracle story.

While in Alaska, I injured my back. I was laid up in bed for two solid weeks barely able to move. When I was able to stand upright again, it was obvious my spine was severely damaged. When we got back to Wisconsin, I went to a doctor who told me she would be able to help me feel more comfortable, but the radiographs indicated that my spine was both curved and rotated and that the damage would not be able to be reversed. I went to her every week for "adjustments" for nearly a year.

Meanwhile, the left side of my back was growing the "hump" that is common in scoliosis patients, even though I did not have scoliosis. One of my legs was shorter and I was fitted for orthopedic shoe inserts. My left hand tingled and my lower back would often spasm. It was getting to the point where I could not sit for extended periods of time. Walking stairs was a real problem too.

Philippians 4:13 I can do all things through Christ who strengthens me.

I prayed for a cure. The days passed and I figured I had used up all of my allotted miracles in this lifetime (the devil really likes to pull this lie on us, doesn't he?).

I figured I had used up all of my allotted miracles in this lifetime.

Meanwhile, a friend came to visit us from Alaska. She is one of the dearest and strongest women in Jesus Christ I have even known. I truly am blessed with her friendship. She has seen the face of Jesus Christ who saved her life many years ago. While staying with us during an extended holiday in 2015, she noticed the pain I was in and saw the difficulty I had walking.

My friend happens to be an ordained minister. During her visit with us, she became our teacher (we didn't realize it at the time) and explained the Gifts of the Holy Spirit to us and how

Jesus is with us today just as much as He was when he walked the earth with his disciples.

We grew up in Jesus Christ during her time with us.

Mark 16:15-18 And he said unto them, Go ye into all the world, and preach the gospel to every creature. He that believeth and is baptized shall be saved; but he that believeth not shall be damned. And these signs shall follow them that believe; In my name shall they cast out devils; they shall speak with new tongue. They shall take up serpents; and if they drink any deadly thing, it shall not hurt them; they shall lay hands on the sick, and they shall recover.

One Sunday morning during her visit with us, we were sitting at the computer watching the live stream broadcast of the services of her ministry in Alaska when she turned to me and said, "I am going to pray for the healing of your spine." And she did. She laid her hands on my back and prayed in the Holy Name of Jesus Christ and asked Him for healing. I remember during one part of the prayer, she thanked God for all His mercies and love, said that if the ocean was the inkwell and the sky was the parchment, there would not be enough ocean or sky to fill with all of the praise for His Goodness.

When she was finished praying in His Name, she looked at me and told me to raise my arms above my head. I did. My back cracked and popped loudly up into the right side of my head. It continued to pop and crack for the rest of the day. Thank you, Jesus! My back is straight! The hump is gone! My legs are the same length! I am healed!

Thank you, Lord Jesus Christ. Thank you.

Psalm 146:2 I will praise the Lord as long as I live. I will sing praises to my God with my dying breath.

Jesus Christ is my Savior and Lord. As you've read, I am a married woman totally and completely in love with my husband. We have five children collectively (we both had previous marriages), and most of our children do not speak to us. It breaks our hearts even though we stay focused and remind each other this is just another indication of the times we live in today. My husband works over fifty hours a week in an effort to clear the literally million dollars plus we lost when we lived out of state. I know about unfairness in life. It is what it is, and I think every follower of Jesus' biggest hurdle is to not let our hearts get hardened and to not drown in our own tears no matter what.

Today, I am an ordained minister - my parish is on the streets and my congregation is a rag-tag group of warriors who have been healed just like me. In the Holy Name of Jesus Christ, I continue to lay hands on the sick and the elderly - I have seen more Miracles, Healings, Signs and Wonders in the last two years than in my entire life.

I have heard His voice, and I hang around with people who have seen His face. We are powerless without His grace.

Lord Jesus, please bless each and every one of us.

We are powerless without His grace.

Romans12:9-13 Let love be without hypocrisy. Abhor what is evil. Cling to what is good. Be kindly affectionate to one another with brotherly love, in honor giving preference to one another; not lagging in diligence, fervent in spirit, serving the Lord; rejoicing in hope, patient in tribulation, continuing steadfastly in prayer; distributing to the needs of the saints, given to hospitality.

Dr. Martin Luther King, Jr.:

"Faith is taking the first step even when you don't see the whole staircase."

Paula H.

Mayer

Paula H. Mayer is a speaker, Young Life Committee member and aspiring storyteller. After graduating from Ohio State, the Rocky Mountains lured Paula to hike and start her decade long commercial insurance industry career in Denver. She married Rick (now her husband of thirty years)! Together they internationally adopted children from China, Russia, and Kazakhstan. Paula is the survivor of three cancers and a bone marrow transplant. Home is Mequon, Wisconsin, but she enjoys her lake cottage, Germantown Life Church, bible studies, and crafting. Paula hopes to bring encouragement to others through her unique personal stories which you can find at: betweengrit-n-grace.com.

—— Chapter 9 ——

IT'S NOT OVER YET, PEOPLE!

Paula H. Mayer

"I have come that they may have life, and have it to the full."

John 10:10b (NIV)

As I dangle my dainty ankles off the edge of my pier in the sparkling, warm water, I'm quickly reminded of my rescue. I take note of the well healed scars on my left ankle. The scars remind me of the accident's trauma with drama, although it pales in comparison to the events that preceded and followed the September 2014 hiking accident on my descent from Flattop Mountain outside of Anchorage, Alaska. I'd spent a lifetime on the edge.

I had good reason for being out on that mountainside. I had been through some health struggles that needed prayer and, following them, when I returned to my life on the mountains, a relative had asked me why did I do such a stupid thing? "I was with you in prayer, till you went off and did that stupid hike!"

> *What did he cover me in prayer for? So I could live life in a bubble?*

What did he cover me in prayer for? So I could live life in a bubble? After all, I was declared in remission from cancer on October 30th, 2014 and I don't think I was saved to play it safe. Hiking by myself on an easy three and a half mile hike with just 1500 feet of gain, on a heavily traveled trail, had seemed a logical goal.

I had been an experienced mountain hiker, starting from the time I was just nineteen and including hiking the front range of the Rocky Mountains outside of Estes Park, Colorado and climbing 14,000-foot peaks. My thirst to conquer mountains during my college summers goes back to my need to over-compensate for what I thought was a negative: being shy and introverted in my young years. Hey, it put "grit" in my life to allow me to be an overcomer in other areas of my life such as, taking on drama roles in early high school, then followed by career risks. After marriage, the pattern continued with three independent international adoptions from China, Russia and Kazakhstan, that weren't for the faint at heart. Mountain climbing had become my impetus to push myself to achieve goals, not to mention getting a natural physical (and literal) high! I feel spiritually in tune when climbing mountains and often reflect on the many metaphors in the bible that pertain to the subject of mountains.

In a nutshell, I climbed Flattop to achieve a goal while I was nearly in remission from Mediastinal Large B Cell Lymphoma, a rare cancer.

On the descent from my goal-aiming hike, I had an unfortunate slide down loose scree and ended up with a left ankle fracture. I tried to keep calm and hop down a trail head, but crumbled in exhaustion and defeat. While I was crawling, a former army medic and, coincidentally, a former nurse, came to my assistance. Another man hiking up the trail stopped near us. He felt that a $5,000 helicopter rescue was out of the question. The three rotated turns doing the "two-person seat carry method".

In the interim, they called 911 to get the park ranger and he came via an ATV, as far as he could drive, and then had me ride piggy back the rest of the way back to the ATV, in order to give the others a rest. I was numb, but had my wits about me to realize here I am being met and rescued by a nurse and, every girls dream, a handsome Prince Charming, my ranger (although he wasn't as cute as my husband, Rick)! I noticed that he was wearing cologne in, of all places, bear country! My own Prince Charming, my husband, met us in the parking lot and, after a quick heartfelt thank you to all involved, he whisked me away to the University of Alaska Hospital to get my swollen fracture casted. My surgeon in Milwaukee told me that the effects of the chemotherapy had weakened my bones, and thus, the serious break required a long plate and several screws in various places for stabilization. My Milwaukee oncology team was surprised to say the least. But, they shouldn't have been. After all, they'd seen me through far more than a little tumble down a mountain.

On January 3, 2014, I found Rick, my oldest daughter, Madeline, and I starring in a movie we couldn't escape. I thought I was having a heart attack while working on my computer. I yelled for Madeline to drive me to the emergency room. My neck and face had quickly swollen. I knew this was bad. In hindsight, I had a chest cough for a few months, but had ignored it. I had my college-aged daughter racing through stop signs to get to the hospital. Rick quickly met up with us. That day, I knew our lives would be forever changed.

It wasn't a heart attack. Instead, I had a thirteen centimeter tumor in my chest cavity. It was surreal to look at the X-ray. I didn't cry, rather I thought NOT, *'why me, God ?'*, but *'why not me?'* After all, I'd lived already to an amazing fifty-four years and had seen a cousin and niece tragically pass away prematurely in their youth, plus many other cohorts and relatives. I recalled my mother, who was in the late stages of Alzheimer's. She would sadly, but perhaps a blessing, never know my prognosis and what was just beginning to lay ahead in the years to come. Rick quickly mobilized an effective and extensive e-mail prayer chain. Soon, an amazing outpouring of cards, meals, prayer healing service with the anointing of oil, gifts, house cleaning, people looking out for our children in creative ways, and car rides came our way.

It was humbling to allow the community and Body of Christ to go to work for our family. I remember a friend said to Rick and I that people would "be watching us" and I thought, *'Oh great! Now I feel I have to put on my happy face. Here we go.'*

The question of, *'why not me?'* from the start paved the way for acceptance.

I sobbed the next day when I realized the prognosis was not good due to the bulky size of the tumor. I wondered how long the thirteen centimeter, wet, sloppy tumor had been residing in me.

In September of 2013, I had spent two years training to climb Long's Peak, a 14,000-foot peak in Colorado, a very difficult sixteen miles round trip climb with a 5,000-foot gain. The purpose of the climb was to have a memorial service on the summit to scatter my dear friend's husband's ashes with his wife and close friends. I almost summited, but I believe God told me to not risk the ice on the last stretch. The others went ahead. I did not have altitude sickness, but didn't have the burst of energy to crawl up hand and foot the last slippery stretch. Another friend stayed back with me for awhile, but preceded ahead. I traveled back the long hike through thunder and hail. All that time, I had been overcome with a blood cancer and a large mass developing in my chest cavity. Oxygenated blood is crucial for high altitude climbs.

My oncology team was aggressive to take life-saving measures in my very first week of diagnosis; they immediately started treating dangerous blood clots in my neck while implementing chemotherapy to knock down the growing tumor. The regiment required six nights and seven days of inpatient hospitalization chemotherapy with twenty-one days off for a total of six cycles. What was in my favor? I was under age sixty and physically fit with no preexisting conditions or medications. What wasn't? The size of the bulky tumor was concerning.

I believed at the time that, by the grace of God, Long's Peak saved my life, but more importantly the prayers from all over the country and world were going to intervene. I realized I had a marathon climb ahead and not just a sprint; it would require my God given grit mixed with trust. One of the nurses closed the door behind her and asked me why hadn't she seen me cry? She felt led to share her story of how her teenage daughter ten years ago had lost her life and she was concerned that I was too stoic. I was given permission to let down my guard...to let down my grit. Together, we cried and I confided with her that the night before I tried to pray and talk with God, but I groaned as I didn't have the words.

The Lord allowed me to escape into His lap, as I sobbed for not me, but my family. After six months of cycling through chemotherapy, living with a swollen face from high doses of chemo, and a bald head, I ended up with a residual tumor of great concern. The fact that I was going to have six weeks of full chest radiation was almost non-existent with this type of chemo.

> *The Lord allowed me to escape into His lap...*

The words I needed to pray to God, the words that were merely groans before, came to me anew:

Moses and the Israelites faced what they thought was an impossible situation caught between the evil one and the Red Sea.

God promised the Israelites a way out and he protected them through dangerous paths of uncertainty regarding their fate. God allowed them to become trapped between the enemy's army and the Red Sea. The God who led them in would lead them out.

I knew God could continue to do that for me and as he did the past year as he'd fought for me. Exodus 14:14 says, *"The Lord will fight for you; you need only to be still."*

My family and I began to live life with a new lease. I traveled along with Rick to Alaska while he attended an Orthopedic conference with his doctor customers in September 2014. It was a trip full of life to the full. I got to zip-line in the tundra outside of Denali National Park. Then, it was my day to climb. It was in Alaska that I fractured my left ankle. But, after I received my cast, I continued my trip in a wheel chair on a sea cruise out to the glaciers. It was a blessing we were with orthopedic doctor friends on our trip for advice. The emergency room doctor also prayed with me, knowing my recent history. When we got back to Milwaukee, I had surgery and used a scooter to get around with a walking cast. Rick planned an epic family vacation to New York City for the day after Christmas and to witness the dropping of the New Year's Eve ball at Time Square. I was able to hobble along in my walking cast for miles a day. It was a magical time for our family!

At the end of April 2015, Rick and I got the phone call every parent dreads, our child was in the hospital with a serious burst fracture to her spine. It was a close call, but no paralysis. Maddy was in school at Xavier University in Cincinnati and Rick and I had to tag-team over the next three weeks for her surgery and recovery, and then move her back to her apartment where she would finish her finals a week late. Again, the prayer chain was activated by Rick with a weekly request of specifics. I headed down to assist Maddy in getting to her nursing finals and help her move out of her apartment back to Milwaukee. I lived with her and her roommates for two weeks all while I was dealing with fatigue, emotional strain and a serious developing fever. I called my oncologist team and they wanted me to go to a Cincinnati emergency room to see what kind of infectious disease I had. I told them I was too busy to arrange an appointment with an infectious disease specialist in Ohio and I needed an appointment the day I got back in Milwaukee. They were not too happy to say the least.

In Milwaukee, an infectious disease specialist ran every test on the face on the earth trying to identify the source of fever. The next day I went to see him and he told me the lymphoma was back; he picked up the phone and called my oncologist. I went home that night with trepidation while developing excruciating pain in my abdomen. Rick rushed me to the emergency room. My medical team was shocked that I lit up like a Christmas tree on a PET scan with a tumor blockage in my upper bowel. I was diagnosed with therapy related Acute Myeloid Leukemia (AML) which was aggressive. It's unheard of to have therapy related AML develop in such a short time, as it doesn't typically show up for five to fourteen years past treatment. My aggressive radiation treatments had caused the condition.

Therapy related AML requires immediate life saving measures with chemo and an allogeneic bone marrow transplant. It was a race against the clock to save my life. I was hospitalized in June of

2015 to start consolidation chemo for several weeks. It was during this time my mother passed away from Alzheimer's and my son, Zach, graduated from High School. I was despondent as I missed the memorial and burial of my mother, as well as Zach's graduation. There was little relief in knowing that my mom, eight years into a progressive Alzheimer's, had been too far gone to have witnessed my own sufferings. That suffering included the search for a bone marrow donor.

When we first found out that my family was going to be reviewed, the odds were a twenty-five percent chance that we would have a half or full match. We ended up having a perfect match. It was the ideal scenario. Over the course of several very precious weeks, my medical team worked with the donor and things were running fine. Unfortunately, there was a lot of misinformation about the procedure of donating bone marrow still floating around out there online. The risk was not one that my full match donor was willing to take. My relative pulled out. The change from this full match would become relevant later.

We were devastated. I had to go back into chemo-therapy just to stay alive long enough while in a holding pattern in wait for a new donor. Precious time had been lost. Sand was falling out of my hourglass like loose scree down a mountainside. The entire experience caused excruciating emotional pain within our family, added to the already present physical pain in my body. There was confusion and a scramble to find a donor. My youngest sister was a half match (haploidentical) and we had to run with her gracious offer to be my donor. It was strange that my highly favorable ethnicity did not lead to one match on the world wide international donor list. It was unheard of.

Why God, do I keep falling into these dismal rare statistical situations?

What are you telling me God?

God, are not even you powerful enough to rescue me when, historically, you have literally carried me down the sides of mountains?

My donor, traveled out to Milwaukee in September of 2015 to get ready to become my living blood. In the midst of her medical test and procedures with the bone marrow team, we had a week where I was out of the hospital and stabilized to enjoy a beautiful fall, touring and playing in the farmlands and charming towns outside of Milwaukee and the city's urban tourist offerings. Fall is my favorite season and I felt so alive and scared at the same time.

In the midst of thinking about the unknown ahead, I had a false sense of theology. I talked with God and said, *'surely God, you wouldn't take me out of the picture at this point since my children have already lost connection with their birthparents. How could you take away their adoptive mom? God, you wouldn't do that.'*

This was my bargaining with God. Hannah did it in the bible when she was infertile. I also bargained with God when Rick and I were desiring to be biological parents and adoptive parents. When we were living with early young adulthood affluence, I bargained with God to take it away as it was not making us happy, when so many of our friends were financially struggling at the time, but having families. God if you gave us a child, I'd live in a garage and train our child in the ways of the Lord. I just trusted that God knew our hearts as he knew Hannah's desire for a son as she made promises to God.

In October of 2015, one million cells from my sister were implanted in me. My team felt one million cells was sufficient. After the transplant, Amy went home, and we were optimistic to see my daily gradual blood counts increase during my five week stay in the recovery unit. I started out of the gate with slow daily gains and some days, no gains. It wasn't until after three weeks that the team was hopeful a successful graft would take place. A successful graft is a life or death point in the game.

I was home by November and was looking to enjoy my fall, with Thanksgiving around the corner. Two of our children, Maddy and Zach, had been in college during this time and Mira, our youngest daughter, was in high school. I even wanted to host Thanksgiving!

Around the end of November, though, I was back in the hospital for a week or two as my platelet count was slipping; it was a sign I'm not grafting. I took a turn for the worst and developed the BK Virus (named BK after the man who discovered the virus) due to a chemo suppressed immune system. Essentially, the virus, stemming from imperfect matches that don't graft as well, caused me to hemorrhage and drop in platelet count. Over a two month period, which included Christmas and New Years, I would go in for daily platelet transfusions. My friends came to my rescue the best they could by staffing a daily presence of caregivers along with home health care nurses. I was deathly ill and needed to be hospitalized again. I had an unheard count of a billion copies of the BK virus in my body. I miraculously pulled through and was stabilized by Christmas.

I continued my weekly platelet transfusions into late winter in order to survive and was given chemo to the bladder to kill the BK virus. I needed a second stem cell collection from my sister. Amy came to Milwaukee in April of 2016 to donate and she surprised the medical team by providing six million cells! It was a game changer.

After grafting, a research doctor walked in my room to check up on me during rounds. I hadn't seen him but once before, but knew he was a follower of Jesus. I wasn't expecting to see him, but he smiled as he walked in and asked me how I was doing? He asked, "When are you going to write your book?" I laughed. It wasn't the first time I'd heard that given my last two years' experiences.

He listened, and smiled, and I felt I had made a personal connection with him. He attended a church I was familiar with and I had met his daughter on the floor who was my Patient Care Assistant. Typically, my doctors had been all business due to their limited time, but he lingered. I asked him why did you ask me, "when am I going to write my book?"

He said, "Well, you have defied the medical odds on several fronts not only surviving two cancers, but the BK virus too!"

It dawned on me he wanted me to know the significance of my scenario from the perspective of my being a believer.

I asked, "Are you telling me this because I'm a medical marvel or because God intervened in a miraculous way?"

Are you telling me this because I'm a medical marvel or because God intervened in a miraculous way?

He just smiled while wandering out the room. I sat alone without interruptions for about an hour, which is unusual due to the hourly nursing checks in the rooms. I had privacy for a change! I was alone praising God while weeping. I realized it took facts from a research doctor to convince me it was a miracle that I was alive at this point. I guess it's the way I'm wired, that I needed proof of the unbelievable. God brought me out from death.

Over the next few days I had many conversations with various medical and staff workers about my dismal statistical numbers to see if they were surprised. One doctor couldn't believe how, every time I was punched down, I miraculously rose again time after time. I thought God brought me through the Red Sea to safety. During those few days, I felt I had a captive audience to question and share my story.

After my booster bone marrow transplant, I had many therapy-related setbacks, including more ICU hospitalizations due to blood clots and a blood septic infection the spring of 2017. I was still able to drive, shop, wine and dine, socialize, and host a few parties. Maintaining the rhythm of life is good. Rick and I set another goal of making a family trip with three other families to Montana and to visit a few National Parks along the way. I had one last surprise early spring of 2017. I noticed some sores on my chest and back weren't healing and I was diagnosed again with cancer. Can you believe that? It was squamous cell skin cancer that required Mohs surgery. It's discouraging to get another therapy related cancer due to radiation therapy. God does provide hope all along the way. I developed Graft Versus Host Disease (GVHD) that causes chronic pain, but my medical team has me on a photopheresis treatment plan.

As I pull my ankles out of the warm sparkling clear water from my pier, I'm reminded how I've been rescued many times in the past several years. In hindsight, I look back and see the fingerprints of God all over my life.

One recent new doctor looked at my chart and said, "I see you've been busy just trying to stay alive" after I apologized for not getting to her sooner. I thought to myself that my last three and a half years of life have been worth it if I can get one person to fight to the end. When the research doctor asked me, "when am I going to write my book?" I realized that what was holding me back is that I didn't want to be defined by my cancer. I had so much other material in my life to share. It's somewhat of a mini- miracle that I'm even writing a short story chapter because my giftedness is not being a writer. I climb mountains!

At a family Christmas gathering as few years back, one of the children, Samuel, played *Oh Come Little Children* on his violin for entertainment. During one of the song's repeat choruses, an elderly relative grew inpatient and starting clapping. The child stopped, looked at the audience and said, "it's not over yet, people!" We all stopped in our tracks, chuckled and continued to listen. That funny moment always makes me laugh because the bold child surprised and then captivated the audience. He was in control of the situation.

Samuel's statement reminds me of my story. God put me here to live life...and live it to the FULL. He didn't save me to live in a bubble. I'll continue to hike the paths he puts before me. I've heard God loud and clear saying, "it's not over yet, people!"

Steve Jobs:

"Sometimes life hits you in the head with a brick. Don't lose faith."

KIMBERLY
JOY
KRUEGER

Kimberly Joy Krueger is the Founder of The Fellowship of Extraordinary Women (FEW), biker chick, lover of God, and a patriot. She is the author of "FREE!", "Parents are Leaders", and co-author of "The Ah-Ha Effect". Whether writing, speaking, or coaching, she lives her purpose by empowering women to live extraordinary lives and tell their stories. Kimberly resides in Mukwonago, Wisconsin, with her husband and best friend, Scott, and four of their twelve children. With seven sons and five daughters, there is never a dull moment. She loves being 'Noni' to her five grandchildren and will tell you the grandparent club is the BEST club she has ever joined! For more information on FEW and Kim, please visit: kimberlyjoykrueger.com.

—— Chapter 9 ——

MY MAGNIFICENT MONKEY WRENCH

Kimberly Joy Krueger

"A determined soul will do more with a rusty monkey wrench than a loafer will accomplish with all the tools in a machine shop."

ꌗ*Robert Hughes*

"That car is going to hit you." Like a monotone version of James Earl Jones, my mind narrated the terrifying scene unfolding before me as if I weren't the one experiencing it.

"It just hit you," James went on. "Now you are on the hood of the car. Now you are in the air." And finally, a few seconds later, "Okay. You've landed on the pavement."

Safe to say, 'on the pavement,' wasn't remotely where I expected to find myself on that beautiful, Florida morning. Being that I was there on vacation, 1,400 miles from my home in Wisconsin and from all twelve of my kids, you could say that getting hit by a car was quite the monkey wrench! I had no idea when I went out for my run that morning how my life was about to be changed. Forever...*for the better.*

The Longest "Vacation" Ever

When my husband, Scott, and I headed out for our annual Florida getaway in late October of 2014, we expected ten days of sunshine, the crashing of ocean waves, and long romantic walks on the beach. Instead, we got weeks of harsh fluorescent lights, the crashing of a '67 Firebird into my poor, unsuspecting body, and romantic wheelchair rides from rehab to the hospital cafeteria.

On the eighth of our ten-day trip, I woke early to go for a five-mile run. I left my father-in-law's beautiful winter home before he, Scott, and my mother-in-law had awoken. I expected to get back before they even knew I was gone. I also expected to successfully cross that street less than one mile from their home, but that didn't happen, either.

Just seconds before I ran across that intersection, I thought about how great it was going to feel to get my run in early as I silently thanked God that I wouldn't have to run in that stifling, mid-day, Florida heat. I anticipated a day of sunbathing on the boat as I allowed the sights in pristine Lemon Bay to take my breath away. As I crossed the intersection, thinking it was "all clear," I very quickly heard monotone James Earl Jones tell me it very much wasn't. Thus, my ten-day trip turned into a one-month stay and went down in my family history as the longest (and most expensive!) vacation ever.

Pavement Revelations

I have a confession to make: I tend to be quick-tempered. It's been a weakness my whole life and I suspect I'll be working on it until Jesus comes back. I'm getting much better at reeling myself in when it comes to unleashing on others, but I am still lightning fast at blasting myself. I've been my toughest critic for the better part of my life and hey; it's a hard habit to break. Although I have made great strides over the years, that morning on the pavement was NOT one of those times. At least not at first.

After James kindly let me know that I just did a face plant on the pavement, it took a second for me to fully absorb what had happened. When I finally did, a singular emotion, accompanied by a sensation of heat, flooded my body.

I was *ANGRY*!

I knew enough in that moment to realize that I was completely conscious. In fact, I was exceptionally alert and awake, and definitely not in shock—which was why I was so mad!

'Who stays awake for this?' I asked myself. *'Wow! Way to go, Kim! You couldn't even manage to be knocked unconscious while being hit by a car? That would've made all this A LOT easier you know! Leave it to you to even do THIS the hard way.'*

As quickly as these thoughts came, they were interrupted. It was as though God deliberately stepped into my head and responded to me like the parent of a two-year-old in the middle of a fit.

"And do you know why you are conscious and wide awake?" God asked me.

'Hmmm, because I don't have a brain injury?' I reasoned. I reasoned! Wait a minute. I could reason! I still had all my faculties! I had been hit...by a car. A CAR. And I was okay!

I had been hit...by a car. A CAR. And I was okay!

Then it came: a deluge of peace. The peace of God flooded my soul more powerfully than any Florida ocean wave ever could. He spoke right to my heart:

'You're in the middle of a miracle.'

Humbled by the power and Presence of God, and sensing I was somehow chosen for this, I responded, *'Well, then...I guess this is the next thing we're doing together, Lord.'*

I had no idea what "this" was going to be and things were happening fast. The God-interruption to my thoughts was also interrupted. This time, it was something physical, not spiritual; the delayed response to my injury. As soon as God and I got things straight, the sensation of one thousand knives (or any other medieval weapon that comes to your mind) ripped through my right leg. I cried out in agony, "My leg, my leg!"

When I'd been hit, I landed with what I now know must have been quite a crunch, crumpled motionless onto the right side of my body. I was in the middle of a piercing, cutting pain in my right hip that emanated down my right leg. It pulsed and burned and cut all at once; sharp and piercing and—although there was no blood—I felt thoroughly bloodied.

"DON'T MOVE!" people were shouting at me. "You shouldn't move!"

In pain and powerless to move or even attempt to make an adjustment to better my situation, I could only try to observe my situation. I listened and watched while I continued to lay wrapped up in the stink of my running clothes, thick with the stubborn scent of the countless runs they'd endured. There's no way to really wash away that smell.

Sometimes, when I run, I like the sensation of taking in the world without filters. On this day, I went without glasses or contacts. I could see well enough around me, but now everything was blurry. A crowd began to gather around and, between my lack of glasses and my required motionlessness, I was at their mercy. I didn't know who was there, who was touching me, what vehicles were going by, who was staring. I could see only one direction, parallel with the sidewalk and I may as well have been laying there completely nude for as vulnerable as I felt.

To my surprise, A woman calmly urged me, "Please don't move, I'm a nurse. Help is on the way. Where else does it hurt?"

Another introduced himself, "I'm an off-duty EMT. We've already called 9-1-1. They will be here any minute."

'Seriously, God? A nurse and an EMT on this random corner?' It's like he was winking at me while I lay on the pavement. Still, it seemed to be taking an awfully long time for actual help to arrive.

The nurse and EMT began to assess my injuries as I simultaneously assessed the reality of my situation. I came to this conclusion: "No one has been told I'm here right now! At least no one I wanted to be told!"

"I want my husband! I NEED my husband!" I had turned into the child who falls off of a bike and is crying out for her parents. Except, instead of pleading for 'mommy' and 'daddy', I cried out, just as illogically, for my husband. "I need my husband!" I kept saying. Every moment without him there was suffocating.

I began to cry out for someone to call Scott only to remember that the whole house was asleep and his phone was always off when he slept. "Never mind…it will do no good. His phone is powered off!" I pictured him sleeping peacefully less than one mile from this scene where I so desperately needed him…it may as well have been a million miles. He was so close, yet felt worlds away. I helplessly cried out for someone to call my father-in-law's landline. He could tell Scott!

"Please call my father-in-law!" I begged.

They asked, "What's his number?"

Who knows people's numbers anymore?

"It's in my phone!" I declared. That is when I realized that my phone was in my arm carrier—*and I was laying on it.* Ordered not to move, there was no way to call the landline. But wait! I know Scott's number…and back to the reality that his phone is turned off. I was caught in a loop.

More voices came around and behind me: "What hurts?" "Where were you hit?" "What happened?" Different voices, but the same concern in each one.

"WHERE ARE THEY?" I heard somebody saying into a phone. "We called 9-1-1 a long time ago! Why aren't they here yet?"

The person sounded panicked. Then, the same voice would try to console me. I heard them freaking out, so it wasn't working! In my head, it didn't matter, anyway. I wanted the people who could really help me: I don't mean, physically, but my support system. I wanted my husband, my family, my friends.

When the ambulance arrived, I begged them to call Scott. But they didn't call. Their priority was me.

When I got to the ER, I begged them to call. They didn't call either. Something about taking care of me, first.

At the local hospital, the tests, poking, and prodding began. So did the pain meds, thank God! I was able to ask for my phone out of the band that had been cut from my arm and was on the other side of the room. I finally called my in-law's house myself.

My mother-in-law, Ardy, answered the phone out of a dead sleep.

"Hi, Ardy, can I please talk to Scott. I have an emergency."

"Oh," she said as groggy as I felt under the influence of the sweet pain drugs. "What's the matter?"

"Ardy, I'm at the hospital. I need to speak to Scott."

"At the hospital? Oh, that's right. You really weren't feeling that well last night."

'What?' I thought. 'I was fine last night.'

"I'm not sick, Ardy. I was just hit by a car and I'm at the hospital. I really need Scott on the phone."

In a moment, she seemed to wake up and Scott was put on the phone.

"I was just hit by a car. I need you now. Right now."

"I'll be right there," he said and he was by my side in no time.

By phone, Scott thought I seemed okay...and then he saw me. He realized, 'She's not okay, and we're in for a bumpy ride before she is, again.'

The medical team ordered X-Rays, expecting to find a broken right leg. Upon their return from reading the results, they announced, "Well, young lady, you've earned yourself a helicopter ride because we can't help you here. You are being flown to a trauma center in St. Petersburg! We thought you had a broken leg, but your leg is fine. You actually broke your pelvis—pretty badly—and you're going to need surgery to fix it."

The helicopter and two-man flight crew had already arrived and were waiting in the hallway.

Spike and Alex

Before I tell you this part, I just want to say that by now, the drugs had really kicked in. And in my own defense, they were pretty strong! That had to be the reason I did what I did and said what I said when I met Spike and Alex. As the nurse rolled me out into the hallway to meet my new escorts, two unique, striking (and handsome!) men were there to greet me. Both were in flight suits, but that was not the primary thing that stood out as they introduced themselves to me.

"Hi! I'm Spike and this is Alex. I'm gonna get you to the trauma center and Alex—he's gonna be your drug dealer. Alex's job is to make sure you feel no pain on this trip. *You're gonna love Alex.*"

Truth is, I already loved them both. *A little too much.* Spike had platinum blonde hair (spiked, of course), was inked from head to toe and very pierced. Alex was equally as commanding in his appearance only with dark hair (not spiked). They were both, well, ripped. Solid muscle bulged beneath their flight suits. I think one of the nurses actually picked up my chin for me.

"I like your tattoos," I said all gooey eyed, like I had been hypnotized.

Once again, I claim druggedly aggressive on this one. Well, as aggressive as one can be when blind and injured.

"You're in good hands," Spike went on.

Um, duh.

"I can see that," I said in a trance. After staring a bit longer, I managed to completely embarrass myself (without a care, thanks to heavy narcotics). With my husband standing right next to me, I panted like a teenage girl, "You two are the most badass nurses I've ever seen in my life."

With a smile, Spike was quick to correct me. "We're not nurses."

"I don't care what you are." I said, sounding drunk.

Everyone, including Scott laughed. Spike kindly countered my awkwardness by offering to take pictures of the helicopter ride for me. He explained that the only thing I would get to see was the ceiling of his helicopter and what fun is that? He would take some pictures and text them to my phone, or to Scott's; whatever we preferred.

My husband, with the best sense of humor, couldn't resist chiming in at this point. He rolled his eyes and said dryly, "Sure. Kim, just give Spike your number. Take her away, Spike. My work here is done."

We still laugh about my 'Spike and Alex' story. And true to his word, Spike texted us some amazing pictures...to Scott's phone.

God's Favorite Kid

Getting hit by that car made me feel like God's favorite kid. I know, it's a massive contradiction. That is what many of the hospital staff were quick to point out! As I announced with a big smile on my face, that I felt like God's favorite kid, one nurse was stunned. She said with an incredulous stare, "You realize you are lying in a hospital bed…with a crushed pelvis…*after being hit by a car*, right?"

Yes.

I realized that.

Hard not to notice.

Picture this scene with me:
 I'm in a hospital bed.
  I'm 1,400 miles from home.
   I have a shattered pelvis.
    I have six broken ribs.
     I have a head laceration.
      I'm covered in road rash.
       I'm in the worst pain of my life.

My new lot in life, albeit temporary, was as a runner who could not even walk. I was not even able to get up and go to the bathroom. Simply leaning over to get a drink off my food tray threw me into sheer torment with horrific pains shooting down my right leg. Said leg was propped up by two pillows, all day, every day, and—if the pillows began to lose their fluff, even slightly–I felt the stabbing of those one thousand knives all over again. When my body told me it was time to use the bathroom, it was not a "room"…*it was a pan.*

Have you ever used a bed-pan before? Dear Lord, for your sake, I hope not! Well, to use a bed-pan, you must lift your what? (Work with me here for a second.) Your pelvis. Yes, you must lift your (broken) pelvis and then set your (broken) pelvis on a hard steel object. Then you must lift it off again and place it back on the bed. And ten times out of ten, a trip to the bathroom, a.k.a., using the bed-pan, means needing new sheets and a sponge bath. (I won't explain why, you can use your imagination.) In turn, new sheets and a sponge bath mean being rolled over on my what? My hip. The hip that is attached to my pelvis? The hip that just had a small hardware store DRILLED into it? Yes, that hip. Roll to the right, (hold your breath, hold your breath), roll to the left (hold it some more). Oh, and remember that leg that needs to remain perfectly still and strategically placed to stave off those thousand knives and their medieval friends? That leg is coming with us on each of these trips, too.

Simply said, every movement was pure torment.

I began to daydream about the pain of childbirth as if it were a tropical vacation. I begged the nursing staff to just let me have all eleven of my children again instead of this!

"And I'll have all of them in one day," I volunteered. "That would still feel better than this!" I declared.

Yet, I felt like God's favorite kid.

How? Why? What?! From the moment God's peace flooded my soul on the pavement, peace did not leave me. I was completely at rest.

I had NO fear.

I had NO self-pity.

I had NO bitterness.

I was told again and again that, with the "alphabet soup," inside my abdomen, and nature of the accident, I should have had internal organ damage, brain damage, paralysis, or not survived at all. My crushed pelvis should have ruptured my spleen. How was is that not one of those broken ribs punctured a lung? My head hit the pavement, along with the whole right side of my body, but I somehow had no brain injury. And, despite all the bones in my body that had crumpled, my spine was intact and unharmed. I was constantly told it was a miracle. How IRONICALLY PROTECTED I was on that pavement!

I had total acceptance of this new chapter in my life, although at first, I did not have total understanding of why it happened. I had complete peace and then something greater and more powerful accompanied that peace and overwhelmed me. Something I didn't deserve and didn't see coming, but something God decided to unload on me.

It was like a 5K run I once did in a torrential downpour. The race had begun in a light drizzle, but by the second mile, it was raining buckets upon buckets upon buckets! I couldn't even see the other runners around me and we actually listened for the slap of one another's feet in the puddles to be sure not to run into one another. By the time I crossed the finish line, I was fully drenched. It was like water had flooded every pore and I was wet through to my core.

The finish line for my recovery was a long way off, but God got busy drenching me! This time, during the biggest "race" of my life...I got soaked with LOVE! From every which way! I was flooded by it! So much kindness! So much compassion! Every kind thing done for me made me feel loved! Every smile, tender touch, and tray delivered...another bucket of love! Every gentle roll from right hip to left hip...another bucket of love! Every little Dixie cup with pills in it made...another bucket of love! Every pillow fluff, visit from my surgeon, every time my husband walked in the door, I felt God pour out his buckets of love on me. Then came the calls. The texts. The Facebook posts and messages. The emails. The cards. Hundreds and hundreds of them. The flowers and gifts. And the visits. *Yes, visits.* I was 1,400 miles away from home and I still visitors! Buckets upon buckets upon buckets; God drenched me in His love.

See! I told you I was God's favorite kid! I was SO LOVED! I felt loved by the hospital staff, my family, my friends, my clients, and most of all, by Scott.

I know it is annoying when women go on about how great their husbands are, so I will try not to be too nauseating here—but I'm telling you—my husband was INCREDIBLE. From the moment he came to my side, until he cheered me on at my first half-marathon eleven months later, he was incredible. He was tender, kind, and faithful. He cared for me like no nurse ever could. He would jump up to fluff the pillow that was losing its fluff before I even asked him to do so, because he could read the pain level in my eyes. He could tell when I was having a bad day and would proceed to make me laugh (which killed my ribs but I really didn't mind). He took me on multiple 'dates' in my wheelchair, rolling me down six floors to the hospital cafeteria for "dinner and a movie." They had a big screen TV in the dining area and he always made sure I had the best seat in the house. He read my mind (readily) and he tended to my heart (tenderly). He cheered me on and told me I was amazing and inspiring every day. To say, 'I felt loved,' is an understatement.

When we finally got to go home, he showered me, dressed me, fed me, did all the errands, grocery shopped and drove the kids around for me—for months. He took me to appointments, did the laundry and didn't go to bed until my needs were met. All while working full time!

Scott took me to see a movie almost every Saturday afternoon, during one of the coldest Wisconsin winters on record. He'd pull up to the theater entrance and he'd jump out of the car to begin our routine. First, he got my wheelchair out of the back, opened my door and then ever so carefully, helped me from the car to my chair. **Never, not once, did he cause me pain during this routine.** Then he rolled me indoors where it was warm, went back out into the cold to park the car, and then returned with a smile. He parked me in the handicapped section, set the brakes, adjusted my leg and my pillows until I was as comfortable as possible and then we watched the movie of my choice—all to help me get my mind off the pain.

We received home cooked meals for three months. Our freezer was FULL. We were blessed with gift cards for pizza, more visits, and flowers. Dear and precious women came over to study the Bible with me, tended to my fireplace and even took my dogs out.

I'm telling you, I felt like God's favorite kid.

It was as if God and the devil entered some kind of crazy contest—maybe a tug of war of sorts—for my heart and mind. No, not just my heart and mind. It was much bigger than that. I think this war was for my destiny! It's like they both knew they were going to have to bring their A-game. So, the devil pulled out his best weapons: kill, steal, destroy. Then God pulled out His best weapons: Peace. Joy. And LOVE.

And Love took the win. Hands down.

Big Destiny; Big Opposition

And a war for my destiny it was. About ten days into my hospital stay, God graciously revealed what was going on behind the scenes. He didn't have to. I didn't even ask Him why. But He told me, and he did it through my own mouth. Some dear friends that live in "St. Pete" came to visit and we got to talking about spiritual things. I said something to encourage them and, as soon as I said it to them, I knew it was for me, too. I felt a burning in my heart when the words came out of my mouth. It was like I nailed it, but I wasn't even aiming!

"Remember, in the wilderness, our trials are to test us to see what is in our hearts. But you're not in the wilderness, you are in your Promised Land. And in the Promised Land, every battle is for your inheritance. This battle is for your destiny! You're not being tested; the enemy is trying to keep you from God's Promises for your future."

So that is what happened in the middle of that intersection on that fateful day?!

Yes. God said, *"Yes."*

As I prayed and talked this out with God later, He reminded me that just two weeks before my accident, I launched *The Fellowship of Extraordinary Women (FEW)*, which was probably the single most powerful extension of my destiny to date.

"You can tell the size of your destiny by the size of your opposition," The Holy Spirit reminded me. I had heard that in a sermon once.

Hmm. I launched a network for women who wanted to live extraordinary lives in Faith, Family, and Business, and two weeks later, I got hit by a car? The devil literally put a hit out on me! This did not scare me. It didn't even intimidate me. *It excited me!* The size of my opposition was evidence of the size of my destiny. Whatever the future held, it was going to be GOOD and it was going to be BIG! But for now, I had to focus on healing.

God's Promises + Your Grit = Miracles!

Sometimes miracles are instantaneous. Those are awesome. I love those. However, I've had very few of those in my life. Often, my miracles have come from a tried and true formula I call "God's Promises plus your grit equals miracles." Can you relate? The miracle I needed after my run in with a '67 Firebird was going to fit that bill, too.

So, I decided to dig in, believe, and persevere. I declared that I was going to be in the best health of my life when all was said and done. While in the hospital, I also announced that I would run a half marathon in eleven months (to everyone's dismay). Today, I can humbly and joyfully declare, I did not lie. Both things came to pass because of my faith in the Word of God and a lot of hard work. A LOT of hard work: physical therapy, training, nutrition, sleep, water, walking, strength training and believing. *Yes, believing counts as hard work, too. Especially on the painful, tired, discouraged days.*

Inspired by my newfound grit, I ran a full marathon, as well as many other half marathons and 5Ks after my recovery. I think I have ten or twelve medals now and only one of them is from before my accident. The conviction to fight harder for my destiny has born much fruit in my mission to serve women, too.

FEW now offers monthly meetings in two cities, has hosted retreats in two states, and offers leadership courses and international publishing opportunities for women! Something else I didn't see coming—in 2017 I launched another business, sharing health and nutrition with whoever will listen. This accident and recovery qualifies me to coach women to live extraordinary lives in mind, spirit and, now, *body*.

My magnificent monkey wrench was a puzzle piece in my purpose I didn't realize was missing—and my life is better for it. I think it's safe to say that Jesus and I are winning the war for my destiny.

The Next Thing We're Doing Together

I'm convinced that Jesus is dead set against being boring—that is why there will always be a "next thing" to do with Him. Okay, maybe (definitely) there is more to it than that, but I choose to accept that I will face new battles for my inheritance in His Kingdom. Something that is different since my magnificent monkey wrench is the attitude I take with me to the frontlines. It's the one I acquired while lying on that pavement:

"Okay, Lord, I guess this is the next thing we're doing together."

Recently, when faced with a brand-new battle, I even shocked myself when saying this to a close friend:

"What's the worst that could happen? So, I get a miracle every five minutes again, so what?"

What? Who said that? Was that me? I promise you, that was the new and improved me. The old me would have went straight to anger. (You know, that quick-tempered thing.) But I am not who I once was because...

Pavement revelations tend to stick.

You're in the mid

dle of a miracle.

Beth Moore:

"If God said it, I want to believe it. If God gives it, I want to receive it. If God shows it, I want to perceive it. If Satan stole it, I want to retrieve it."

SUE

SHERSTAD

Sue Sherstad is an ordained minister, she has been ministering alongside her husband Dan as a team - teaching, preaching and counseling for twenty-five years. Together, they have pastored several churches. Sue shares her personal testimony of "Deliverance from the Pit" to women at churches and conferences to bring hope and restoration to broken lives. Sue's passion is to teach the "Keys that Unlock Prison Doors" from the Word of God to set the captive free and live victoriously for the King! Sue and her husband, Dan, currently reside in Rancho Cucamonga, California, with their two daughters, Danielle and Sarah.

—— Chapter 11 ——

DELIVERED FROM THE PIT OF DESTRUCTION

Sue Sherstad

"Then he said to her, 'Daughter, your faith has healed you. Go in peace.'"

✎ *John 8:48 (NIV)*

*T*here it was again, in the morning as I awoke, that knot in my stomach gripping tightly like a snake coiling around its prey.

I take a deep breath...hold it...hold it...a little longer, now...whooosh...*slowly* exhale. But the knot refuses to let go. It only tightens more. My abdomen is sore from the constant pain of the tension; I proceed to get ready for work. This had become my daily experience - living with chronic anxiety and tormented with fear.

I am a farmer's daughter, the oldest of three sisters with a brother one year older than myself. I was raised on good old-fashioned hard work, from helping with chores in the home to tending the sheep in the pasture. My parents instilled, in me and my siblings, the value of, not just an honest day's work, but also good morals. Because of this upbringing, I held the strong conviction to keep myself pure for my future husband.

After graduating high school in 1975, I set out on my own. I shared an apartment with two girlfriends I worked in a department store in my small hometown. It was in the fall of 1977, as a young, naïve, single, twenty-one year old woman, full of hopes and dreams for the future, that my life took a downward spiral.

I was excited to go out on a date with the nice looking young man who kept coming into my work place giving me his glances and smiles at a distance until he popped the question. I eagerly accepted the dinner invite and looked forward to the possibility of a new and lasting relationship. My high school boyfriend of two years had gone off to college and we felt it was best to date other people.

After a nice evening he said he needed to stop at a friend's house he was watching while they were on vacation before taking me home. I completely understood and said that was fine. He invited me inside and wanted to show me around; I willingly followed. He gave me the tour of the first floor of this nice ranch style home, checking that things were in order. He then led me to the finished downstairs basement, into a bedroom, and shut the door.

That basement bedroom is where my world came crashing in and my innocence was ripped from me. My small and petite frame of five feet, two inches in height and just 105 lbs. was no match to his strength. Ignoring my pleas to stop, he forced himself on me, assaulted and raped me repeatedly in that room until morning. In silence, he drove me home. I was in shock as I stood on the curb, watching his car drive away.

I didn't tell anybody what happened at first; I felt embarrassed and shameful. I really hadn't grasped what had just happened, I actually felt responsible...as if I had caused it. I grieved over what had been stolen from me. It was weeks later before I told my roommates, but it was too late to do anything about it.

Most rape victims are reluctant to come forward because of the stigma, and who wants to lay their life out for everyone to judge? I certainly didn't. The Center for Disease Control, states that nearly one in five women are raped. One of the most striking statistics is that, among women, seventy-nine percent were first raped before the age of twenty-five, and forty percent before age eighteen. Sixty percent of rape crimes are never reported at all, and—when they are—only 6% of rapists serve a day in jail. I fell into this cold and disheartening report of statistics.

Depressed, I started going to disco bars with my girlfriends, drinking alcohol, and experimenting with drugs at parties. I became unrecognizable from the young woman I once was.

This lifestyle was just the beginning of my nightmare life. A couple of months later, I was lying down to take an afternoon nap when something strange happened. It started as a sound, like the roar of a freight train approaching and getting louder. Then an unseen force, very difficult to describe, began to overtake my body pinning me to my bed. My mind was overwhelmed with the loud sound; I lost sense of reality and my surroundings. At first, I wasn't sure whether to be afraid, I felt temptation to give in to the power of the unseen force, as if it was trying to seduce me. Suddenly, I felt fear and, instinctively, I cried out, "Jesus!"

The force broke its hold and the sound diminished. Sitting up, disorientated, as if coming out of a trance, I gradually gained my composure. Not knowing what I had just experienced, I brushed it aside and forgot about it.

It wasn't long before it happened again one night, when I was on the edge of falling asleep. I tried to speak the name of Jesus like before, but I couldn't! I tried and tried to form the words and lift up my voice to no avail. It was as if my face was frozen, as I fought to open my eyes and speak. Helpless, I used my thoughts to resist the overwhelming power coming against me. I kept repeating 'Jesus, Jesus, Jesus,' over and over in my mind, calling upon Him for help. Once more, the force started to lose its grip and dissipate.

I was petrified with fear like I had never known. It was evil. Not knowing what was happening, I wondered, *'Where do I go for help? What do I say, how do I even begin to explain it? People are going to think I'm crazy!'* Keeping it to myself I endured each day and night, locked in a cell of loneliness and fear.

I changed jobs in 1979 and moved to a neighboring town. I lived alone and adopted a puppy for companionship. Having a new job and my own place didn't change anything, though. I dreaded going to bed. *'Would it come tonight?'*

The attacks occurred randomly, maybe once or twice a week. Walking past my own bedroom, fear would grip my soul. Sometimes, I put off going to bed and stayed up late. I began the habit of keeping the light on, afraid of the dark. Restful sleep was a thing of the past. Exhausted, I went to work merely to keep my job.

I developed chronic anxiety, with a constant knot in my stomach. The condition led to panic attacks at work. Those were so humiliating!

Panic attacks at work were different from nighttime terrors. It would happen in front of people, like my boss. My boss didn't know how to respond to me. My heart would begin racing. My face would flush and turn red. It was like an overwhelming emotion; I couldn't think straight when it happened. I couldn't converse properly with people when they occurred. It was the feeling of being out of control of yourself and no power to stop it. That's why they were humiliating. I was at the mercy of this thing happening to me. My department would gather together in a circle and have meetings and that attack would hit me! Then, I couldn't focus on what was being talked about and participate in the conversation. I worried how this made me look to everyone in my department and to my boss. I wondered if they thought that I was not intelligent enough to contribute to the projects discussed.

One time, during an attack, my boss had someone else with him and he came to speak with me at my work station. The panic attack hit me. He didn't understand what was happening to me, so he walked away. Then, I felt Humiliation!

Rejection...

Embarrassment...

Shame. . .A feeling of inferiority.

The person my boss had brought over was a stranger and, somehow, the experience was even more embarrassing because this other person didn't work there. I felt guilty for how I represented my company. I lived in dread of the attacks happening again and it snowballed and built momentum. I was stuck in an overwhelming cycle. Then, I dreaded going to work because I *knew* the horrible panic attacks would come.

Looking for an escape, I continued to party, meeting all the wrong guys. Experiencing more rejection, my soul became deeply wounded. I just wanted to belong and be accepted, but these people did not truly care about me.

I just wanted to belong and be accepted...

This had become my world.

Broken inside and empty, I was a prisoner of fear, stuck in a pit I couldn't climb out of.

Have you ever been in a place where you felt stuck, paralyzed by circumstances or an event in your life? Psalm 40:1-2 Describes being stuck in a pit of destruction and the miry clay. The verse became my story of God's deliverance.

"I waited patiently for the Lord; he turned to me and heard my cry. He lifted me out of the slimy pit, out of the mud and mire; he set my feet on a rock and gave me a firm place to stand."

(Psalm 40:1-2 NIV)

I came to a crossroads late one night in 1981. Walking out of a smoky bar in despair, I sat on the edge of the cold cement curb. Hopelessly I cried, "There's got to be more than this!"

Sick of the bar scene and the broken relationships with multiple men, I drove home.

God was listening that night. I soon got a call from my youngest sister Jeanette, who had found an adorable apartment to rent back in our hometown. She knew the Christian older couple who lived downstairs in this charming Victorian home and was positive I would love the upstairs apartment. Desperate to make a change in my life, I agreed to see it. I fell in love with the open staircase and beautiful hardwood floors. It was an easy decision; the bright, sunny apartment gave me hope for a new beginning. The disco bar scene behind me, I made plans for a fresh start.

I began to attend the Lutheran Church with my parents where I had been confirmed as a teenager. The Pastor's sermons brought the conviction needed for the Holy Spirit to begin molding me and changing me. I felt a new love and hunger for God, like I experienced as a girl in Sunday school. I joined the choir and started teaching the kindergarten Sunday school class. I made new friends in the single's group and enjoyed fun times together.

In spite of all of these wonderful new changes, though, the night terrors continued and the knot in my stomach was persistent.

Seven years had passed since the attacks had begun and I still had no miracle or breakthrough. I wondered, *'Could I speak with my pastor about this, could he help me?'*

Mustering up all the courage possible, I made an appointment. Listening to my story with as much compassion as possible, my Pastor had no answers to my dilemma. Almost embarrassed, I went home disappointed.

Seeking God more in prayer, I cried out to Him, "Lord, send me a strong Christian to help me!!"

And...He did...because that's the God we serve. He answers when we call upon Him. He brought a young man named Bill, who was a friend to my downstairs neighbors. I found out they were doing a little match making. There was something different about him. He spoke of God like he knew him intimately. We became close friends, someone I could trust.

Then, one night I had the most horrible experience ever. It was another night terror, but this time the force or entity manifested over me. My eyes open, I saw a misty dark figure appear above me and the sounds of growling as I lay paralyzed unable to speak or move. Like I had done many times before, I resisted with calling on Jesus in my thoughts. With what seemed like forever, its hold broke and it eventually lifted away.

I quickly looked to see where my little dog was. *'Was it my dog growling?'* No, he was asleep lying next to me.

Petrified I jump out of bed! Something is in this house! I have to get out of here! I grabbed the phone and called the only person I could trust, my friend Bill. I quickly dressed and waited on the front steps for Bill to arrive. Comforting me, he prayed and encouraged me to go back upstairs. As He was leaving, he told me he knew of a pastor who could help me.

Reluctantly, I went back upstairs with all the courage I could find. Still fearful, I slept on my couch and longed for the morning sun to chase away the dark shadows of the night.

I didn't think it could get any worse, but the attacks had escalated to a whole new level. Desperate for help, I went with Bill to meet the pastor he told me about.

It was 1985, when I met the pastor of a small country church in the corn fields. That day, a glimmer of hope filled my heart as this pastor did not give me that blank stare of, *Oh my God, this girl is nuts!* Instead, he calmly looked into my eyes and told me I was in the right place. Not taken back by my horror movie account of night terrors, He encouraged me to attend Sunday morning service. Full of nervous anticipation, I went with Bill to the service. It was different from what I was accustomed to, but I felt something I had never known before. It was what I would later come to understand as the presence of the Lord. I felt a tug in my heart and wanted more. I knew that this was the place to get the help I needed.

I made the hard choice to leave the Lutheran Church. At first, my parents didn't understand my decision, but eventually they came around. A new journey began and I couldn't wait to get to church. The sermons and messages spoke to my heart and I was strengthened and encouraged in my faith. Although I do believe I was saved during my time at the Lutheran Church, for the first time I heard what it meant to be born-again.

I began meeting with my pastor and a counselor every week. It was revealed to my pastor that, as a result of the rape, a demonic spirit had gained entrance into my life. He counseled me concerning spiritual warfare and the demonic realm around us. The Apostle Paul taught the early church that we are engaged in a war against an unseen enemy, the devil.

"For we are not wrestling with flesh and blood, but against the despotisms, against powers, against [the master spirits who are] the world rulers of this present darkness, against the spirit forces of wickedness in the heavenly sphere."

(Ephesians 6:11-12 AMP)

I understood now, as a believer, there was a huge target on my back. I was hopeful, but also overwhelmed by the revelation of what I was up against.

I was in a spiritual battle for my life.

The first major key to freedom was that I had to forgive my attacker. **Forgiveness would release me from the cord of bondage to that trauma and the person connected to it.**

So following my pastor in a prayer, I chose to forgive the man who brought so much pain into my life. A sense of peace flooded over me and I knew something had changed. This was a good start, but my deliverance was going to be a long battle. The demonic attacks still continued and the chronic anxiety persisted. Layer by layer, week after week the Lord ministered to me - His healing in my soul.

There were many Words of Wisdom and Knowledge released by the Spirit, giving direction on how to pray. I remember one session that was extra special. My pastor shared a vision from the Lord for me.

He saw a tall ladder with many rungs which represented my life and my future. I was standing on the bottom rung, when suddenly a laser beam of fire from heaven cut it in half, starting from the top to the bottom. The ladder split and came apart. I fell from the bottom rung and landed on a path below. It was a new path that the Lord had planned for me. The ladder was my past and the future plans of the devil, each rung a designated scheme. Did you know that if you don't seek the Lord for His plans for your life, the devil has his own plans?

But the Lord said, "No more!"

He had a destiny and a good plan for me. The Lord spoke, "You are now washed and cleansed in my precious blood and clothed in white. By My Spirit your virginity is restored."

As a result of rape, I had felt unclean, not acceptable, and not good enough for a future husband. There was a sense of being dirty and that's how I treated myself. I was grieving a loss of purity I once had.

It was not my choice. It was taken. It was *ripped* from me. I was violated.

Have you ever had something broken into and you were robbed? I felt that way, physically. I was broken into and something precious was violently ripped from my life.

And the shame of the rape was overwhelming.

For the Lord to speak in THAT WAY prophetically through my pastor, meant everything to me! My Heavenly Father didn't see me with eyes that said I was filthy. He saw me cleansed and washed in the blood...and I was pure again!

That which was stolen in the natural was now restored by the spirit through redemption in Jesus Christ. I was a new creation in Christ Jesus. The old had passed away and in my heavenly Father's eyes I was made pure again!

"The thief comes only in order to steal, kill and destroy, I came that they may have and enjoy life, and have it in abundance."

(John 10:10 NIV)

My miracle story occurred in two parts. First, being delivered from the demonic attacks thru a process. No instant one time magical prayer and boom it's gone! The second was freedom from the bondage to chronic anxiety.

God has the master keys to unlocking prison doors. After forgiveness, I discovered the next key to my miracle!

"God has not given us a spirit of fear, but a spirit of power and love and a sound mind."

(2 Timothy 1:7)

I heard my Pastor teach from this verse. Up until that point, I had always accepted that fear was a part of life and I had to put up with it. This was simply not true. I realized that fear comes from the devil and I could choose to reject it. Jesus constantly tells us, don't be afraid! So, with this new revelation, I declared this scripture whenever I felt fear come.

As a "baby Christian," I was taking wobbly steps learning to walk. I had good days and bad ones. The battle at night still not won, it was easy to get discouraged. I was so thankful for my dear friend, Carla. She was and is my spiritual mom who I met at church. I could call her anytime for prayer and encouragement after another dreaded attack. She helped to keep me moving forward.

Then, I heard teaching on the Power of the Love of God. This proved to be a turning point to my miracle.

"There is no fear in love (dread does not exist), but full grown (perfect) love turns fear out of doors and expels every trace of terror."

(1 John 4:18 NIV)

My huge breakthrough came when **my faith in His love became bigger than my fear of the enemy** and his attacks. It happened slowly, day by day, as I read the word concerning His love for me. Filling up with His Love, it reached a "tipping point" when suddenly I was no longer fearing the attacks of the devil.

His love became tangible one night.

I could feel God's Presence upon me, while I was sitting on the floor of my apartment, in worship. The weightiness of His Glory wrapped around me like a blanket, it was as if His arms were holding me. I was safe and secure under the shadow of the Almighty. As I received my heavenly Father's perfect love, His peace covered me. He assured me I was His, and He would never leave me or forsake me. Even if the devil came to attack me, I was assured that My Lord would come quickly to rescue me!

During this time my pastor prophesied this verse to me as a Promise from the Lord. To this day it stirs my heart whenever I hear this verse.

*"The Lord is my strength, my personal **bravery**, and my invincible army; He makes my feet like a hind's feet and will make me to walk and make spiritual progress upon my high places of trouble."*

Habakkuk 3:19 Amp.

When the next attack came, I wasn't afraid; **He made me brave!** I rebuked the spirit of fear, commanding it to go in Jesus name!

It obeyed! His name is all powerful and every other name must bow to His name! Demons flee at the mention of His name. Walking in a newfound boldness of authority and assurance of His love, the night attacks weakened...and, eventually... stopped!

I give all glory to the Lord for this mighty miracle! His Perfect Love moves mountains!

My story ends with part two of my miracle. The knot in my stomach refusing to go, I became more determined for my breakthrough. I received new revelation on the Breakthrough Power of Worship. I learned that Praise is like launching spiritual missiles into the heavens that bring down the enemy's strongholds in our lives as in the story of Jehoshaphat.

"As they began to sing and praise, the Lord set ambushes against the men of Ammon and Moab and Mt. Seir who were invading Judah, and they were defeated."

2 Chronicles 20:22 NIV

Inspired to pursue the Lord in worship and trust Him to defeat my enemy, I set aside time on a Saturday afternoon to put this battle plan into action. Putting on worship I bent down on my knees on my hardwood dining room floor before the Lord. My heart determined for a breakthrough, I began to praise Him. Pressing into His Presence, I worshiped for an hour. The knot in my stomach hadn't budged.

With greater resolve, I continued to bombard the heavens with Praise and Worship unto Almighty God! A righteous indignation against the lies of the devil caused me to press in deeper, exalting the Lord and His mighty name!

After praising God for His deliverance for two hours, the supernatural descended upon my small apartment. My arms outstretched in worship towards heaven, the power of God and His anointing hit me. It was like a mighty rushing river, flowing over my head and engulfing my entire body. I felt the sudden release of the grip in my stomach like a tight twisted knot unraveling. I could only sit and be still as I sat kneeling in His Holy Presence. It was precious, a holy visitation of God. *In His Presence is the fullness of Joy and Peace.* I didn't want to move from this place, so I remained, soaking in heavens' atmosphere. When I finally got up, the knot and chronic anxiety were completely gone. I danced and praised God, twirling around in my socks on shiny, hardwood floors.

"You are my hiding place; You protect me from trouble. You surround me with joyful shouts of deliverance."

Psalm 32:7 NIV

Boyd K. Packer:

"Some people think a miracle is only a miracle if it happens instantaneously, but miracles can grow slowly and patience and faith can compel things to happen that otherwise never would have come to pass."

MAUREEN

HURD

Maureen Hurd is a business owner, executive recruiter and leader of a marketplace ministry. She is passionate about helping companies find great talent, and helping leaders integrate their faith at work. She is an emerging author and speaker with bold and authentic messages. Her mission is to inspire hope by sharing her adoption story, life challenges and faith journey. Maureen is married to James and they have two-year old twins. They live in Hartford, Wisconsin and loves connecting through her passions in faith, family, exercise, the outdoors and business. Email her at maureen@coreconnects.com or also at: mhurd@truthatwork.org.

―――― Chapter 12 ――――

A HEART MADE WHOLE

Maureen Hurd

"Yet to all who did receive him, to those who believed in his name, he gave the right to become children of God."

∽*John 1:12 (NIV)*

As I opened my eyes, I was staring at the ceiling. Everything seemed a little hazy. I could still hear voices and soft music. Something had happened. I felt warm, like a charge of electricity had gone through my body.

I was different. A good different, but unfamiliar. An overwhelming sense of peace and love consumed me. My

179

heartache was gone. The brokenness had lifted. What just happened?

As I sat up and looked around the room, there were others on the floor like me. An amazing presence was in the room. The Pastor was praying with someone else who had come forward. Why did I?

An amazing presence was in the room.

There was an altar call for those who needed prayer. I was drawn up to the front of the church, as if someone was taking my hand and saying "Come." The Pastor asked me what I needed prayer for. I didn't know, but God knew. The Holy Spirit knew. The Pastor took my hands and asked, "Do you have a broken heart?" I immediately started to weep, and as I shook my head yes, she started to pray.

I don't remember what she said. All I remember is a warmness rushing through my body. So sudden and all consuming. Unconsciously my body surrendered to this power, my knees buckled, and I fell to the floor.

I believed in the gifts of the Holy Spirit, but hadn't seen all of them in operation. Did I just experience a healing? A miracle? That kind of happening in a church was new to me. I was overcome by the power of the Holy Spirit. The power of God just went through me.

When I sat up, something had changed. I felt emptied. Emptied of the hurt, the rejection, the sadness, the resentment, the anger and the loneliness. I almost felt a little uncomfortable. Not because of the environment or people around me, but because I wasn't the same person who had walked into the church that evening.

I didn't realize the impact of these negative feelings I had been carrying around.

I felt lighter. Peaceful. Content. The weight of emotional burdens lifted.

So now what? Was it just life as usual for me? No! I had a new desire; a hunger to know the Lord…to understand God's Word. As I studied the bible, I was learning about God's love. The love of the Father through His son Jesus Christ. He was taking me to a place of ultimate trust; a new intimacy. For the first time in my life at the age of forty-one, after two marriages and many wrong relationships, I was experiencing an intimate, unconditional love. Obviously, it wasn't a physical intimacy but it was real! I was falling in love with Jesus for the first time. I had believed in and prayed to God the Father, Jesus, His son and the Holy Spirit my whole life and yet never had this kind of relationship. Quite frankly, I didn't know it was available.

God knew what I needed from the moment I was conceived. Jeremiah 29:11 says, *For I know the plans I have for you, plans to prosper you and not to harm you, plans to give you hope and a future.* He knew I was going to need a mom and dad.

My birth parents were teenagers and I was given up for adoption in 1968. God handpicked the parents who adopted me. I couldn't see that growing up, but I do now and I'm very appreciative of who He selected.

They brought me home at four weeks old. We were a simple middle class family. Dad was a carpenter and built houses for a living, and Mom stayed home until I was fourteen years old. I have an older brother and sister. My parents were good and honest people. Their interaction with each other was a great example of a respectful marriage. Mom put the warmth in our home and was the ultimate homemaker. She could bake or sew anything. Dad was a good provider and is a great craftsman, stoic and reserved.

I was baptized as a baby, attended Sunday school, received first communion, was confirmed, and we went to mass every Sunday. I did everything right in my Christian faith journey; everything that was expected of me. But I never felt different. I never felt transformed or that I had a personal relationship with God. I am truly grateful my parents were committed to their religion and laid this foundation for me. It helped keep me on track and accountable to God. I knew Jesus as my Savior. The Holy Spirit thing was more of a mystery.

When I was twenty-one, my mom died from cancer. She was so strong; always positive, never complaining. My dad was right by her side through it all, never showing us his hurt. I rarely saw emotion or received physical love from him. Even the day she died, he held it in. I knew he loved and cared for me, but it was not expressed. I needed that. I longed for a stronger bond and connection with my dad.

As I grew older, a longing in my heart grew more. I wanted to know who my birth mother and father were. Who did I look like? I dreamed about meeting them. Psalm 37:4, *Take delight in the Lord and He will give you the desires of your heart.*

As I grew older, a longing in my heart grew more.

My twenties became an era of wrong relationships. I wanted to be loved and have a deep connection with someone. I tended to blame my dad for dysfunctional relationships. I suppose that was easier than taking responsibility for my own decisions. I chose to hold onto the hurt from his emotional rejection.

For many years, there was a distance between me and God. Not that I resisted Him, or thought He wasn't available. I just didn't have a personal relationship with Him. No one ever showed me or explained to me what that meant.

I accepted Jesus Christ as my Savior at the age of twenty-four, yet still lived with one foot in the world and one foot in my faith. I went to church, and attended bible study. I was walking through the motions, but I made decisions that weren't necessarily God-honoring.

God was doing a work in me and I needed to let him. I needed to let go of the hurt and disappointment from my dad. I had felt unloved, unworthy...like a disappointment, but I had put that there on my heart. My dad never spoke that to me.

I forgave my dad through prayer at the age of twenty-nine. It was a culmination of events that got me to that prayer, from my dating life to my feeling of unworthiness. I had prayed with my head; I had prayed with my heart, but I finally prayed in my spirit and believed it. I finally got to the place where I released everything and cast the care onto Jesus' shoulders. I finally just gave it to God.

Once that happened, my relationship with my Dad did change, but only from my perspective. It got better because there wasn't something between us anymore...the block that I had created. The biggest thing that I wasn't doing God's way was dating. I knew I was supposed to be finding my real mate rather than just dating the way the world expects. Praise God, I chose, at that moment to honor God in everything.

Why was there still a yearning in my heart?

I thought this was a good time to reach out to the adoption agency and start the process to find my birth mother. The feeling of anticipation was overwhelming. I waited and waited for a call. Nothing. I called the agency six months later, and they hadn't processed my application yet. There were many other applications ahead of mine and they didn't know when mine would be processed. Disappointed and discouraged, I eventually forgot about it and moved on.

The summer of 1999, I was engaged and planning a wedding. That's when I got the call. The call I hoped for. The call I dreamed of. The call that would change my life. There was a voice message on the answering machine. I came home from a normal day at work, walked into the kitchen, saw the blinking light and hit play: *"Hello, this is the Catholic Social Services, and we have been successful in locating your birth mother and she wants to meet you."*

I dropped to the floor and was overcome with emotion. I couldn't stop crying. This was a dream come true; an answer to prayer. Oh my gosh, I'm going to meet the woman who gave birth to me! I'm going to find out who my birth father is!

My heart longed to know who they were. I had so many questions. Although I was raised in a wonderful family, there were parts of me that didn't feel connected to them. Isn't that something we all need, to feel connected? A deep desire and longing in our hearts to know we belong, we're loved…accepted. I had that desire and was always in search of it. I thought a person; a family would fill it. Maybe a relationship with my birth mother was what I needed to feel connected.

Her name is Cindy. I received her phone number from the adoption agency and made the call. I was so excited and anxious to speak with her. She was very nice; emotional too. She had longed to know what happened to me. I was an answer to her prayers as well. We talked for a long time about our lives and families.

We met a couple weeks after that; just a month before I got married. My emotional state was full tilt! It was a beautiful reunion. God filled a hole in both our hearts. It was so neat to see parts of me in her. She welcomed me into her family. What a blessing; two younger brothers, a sister, aunts and a grandmother. All of them accepted and loved me like one of their own. Was this the connection I was longing for? Why did I still feel a void?

I learned about my birth father of course. His name is Stan. He was eighteen, and Cindy was fifteen when I was conceived. I was not planned, a surprise to say the least. It wasn't young love, just a one-time "tryst" to describe it simply. Cindy was six months along when Stan found out about me. He easily agreed to give me up for adoption.

I wasn't given a lot of information about Stan. I knew it was painful for Cindy discuss. It was a very difficult time in her life, having to go through a pregnancy at fifteen in the late 1960's. I only learned little about Stan and his family. These two families were close neighbors. Last she knew, he had moved to Fond du Lac to work in construction.

It wasn't much information for me but enough to start a search. I was pretty confident I located his last known address. I didn't really know what to do with the information. I just wrote it on a post-it note and stuck in my desk drawer.

Although my reunion with Cindy was wonderful, she endured a lot of emotional hardship over the years because of her teen pregnancy. **I wanted to honor my relationship with her and my**

desire to find my birth father gradually waned. The post-it note stayed in my desk drawer and remained dormant for many years.

Fast forward to 2007, my husband of almost eight years wanted a divorce. I was devastated. My world was rocked; my heart crushed. I had never felt that kind of pain before. It was all consuming. Like someone stuck a knife in my heart.

'*Why God?*' I was a good wife; a good person. I was going to church and in a women's bible study. I was trying to live a principled life. How could this happen?

I was so grateful to my women's bible study group. They prayed for and lifted me up. They prayed for my husband when I didn't know how to pray for him. Through a business friendship, I got plugged into a coed bible study during this time. All these relationships blessed me. God knew just who to bring into my life.

I was so emotionally spent. I was tired of crying, tired of being lonely, tired of wondering what my life was going to look like. Where was God in all of this?

God was there all the time. He was waiting for me to press into Him; rely on Him. I received His invitation, and went most of the way. I went deeper in my faith and began an amazing faith journey.

I needed Jesus. I needed his saving grace to show me how to forgive. I struggled in my flesh. I picked up the hurt often and had to keep releasing it. God's Word was the only thing that helped me. It was my guiding light and source for help. Forgiveness seemed so unfair. He got freedom without paying for the pain he caused.

The Bible showed me that the act of forgiving would be my seed of obedience to God's Word. Once I sowed that seed of forgiveness, God was faithful to bring a harvest of blessing to me. Mark 11:24-26, *Whatever you ask for in prayer, believe that you have received it, and it will be yours. And when you stand praying, if you hold anything against anyone, forgive them, so that your Father in heaven may forgive you your sins."*

Unforgiveness hindered my faith. I wanted mercy and God's blessing.

I started dating other men, and I made some wrong choices again; still looking at dating from an earthly perspective. Trying to fill that void in my life. I wanted to feel connected to someone again. I wanted an intimate relationship.

In November 2009, I got invited to my girlfriend's church. That evening service changed my future. God healed my heart. After that, I had a deeper desire to know God's Word. I fell in love with Jesus. He became my husband. I was being drawn closer to Him.

I learned to trust the Lord, delight in the Lord, COMMIT to the Lord. He wanted to give me the desires of my heart. I committed every area of my life; fully surrendered my heart, relationships, family, finances, business, ministry and future. It wasn't easy. It was a process, where God kept revealing himself to me. I had the assurance He would provide. Phil 4:19 *My God shall supply all my needs according to His riches and glory through Jesus Christ.*

God knew me so well. He knew there was still one small yearning (hole) in my heart. I believe He wanted to reward my obedience. In December of 2011, that post-it note with Stan's name and address on it popped out, as I was going through my desk drawer. I stared at it for quite a while. Not sure what to do, so I prayed. "Lord, I have surrendered everything to you. You know what I need. I'm trusting you. If I am supposed to meet my birth father, I know you will make it happen."

Just over three months later, I get a phone call from Cindy. She called to wish me happy birthday and said, "I have some news and a special birthday present for you. I just got off the phone with Stan and I have his phone number. He's open to speaking with you."

If standing, I would've dropped to the floor. I was in a girlfriend's car when the call came in. I was immediately overcome with emotion. Oh my God! Cindy cried with me. She knew how important it was to me. What a gift! I had known about Stan for twelve years at this point, and in just three months God created a way for me to meet him.

A couple weeks before the birthday call, Cindy's sisters were having lunch at their hometown restaurant in central Wisconsin. This was about an hour from where Stan lived. He had travelled there with his hunting buddies to look for some hunting land to lease and "they just happened to" stop at the same restaurant for lunch. Now think about what God had to do to orchestrate that. Nothing is too difficult for God!

My aunts recognized him even though it had been forty-three years. Patti approached Stan and said, "Aren't you one of the Johnson boys from Stoughton?" He said "Yes, you are the Barrett girls, right?" He recognized them also.

Patti asked, "What brings you to Montello?"

"I'm here with my buddies to look for hunting land to lease," he replied.

She said, "Well I'm in real estate, here's my card let me know if I can help." They exchanged contact information. Oh what a good God!

Patti shared this information with Cindy. The conversation opened some old wounds. I know it wasn't easy for her to contact Stan. She did it for me. Thank you Cindy!

I had Stan's number and prepared for a life changing call, again. I was anxious, excited and full of gratitude. I'm going to speak to my birth father! Hopefully meet!! This was a scenario that played through my head for many years. I heard his voice on the other end of the phone, "Hello."

"Hi Stan, this is Maureen your birth daughter, Cindy's daughter," I said. I could hear some reservation in his voice, but knew it was going to be okay. He was nice. He told me all about his family and work. He was a proud father and grandfather. The conversation felt very comfortable; familiar.

After about thirty minutes of getting to know each other, I said "Well Stan, I would really like to meet you, and I hope you'd like to meet me, do you get down to the Milwaukee area very often?"

He said, "Not often, but I happen to be going to the Brewer's game this Saturday."

"I'm going to the Brewer's game this Saturday!" I said with excitement.

My girlfriend who had season tickets asked me to be a guest at a game, and she gave me four options. Guess which one I picked!? The Holy Spirit knew which one I should pick; the one my birth father was going to be at.

Yes, we met at a Brewer's game. The anticipation was intense. I was full of emotion, yet felt a sense of peace as well. I felt God's love. This was His handiwork. So many thoughts ran through my mind. What will he look like? What is he going to think of me? Am I going to cry? Should I hug him? How will I find him in the crowd? I hope the Brewers win!

I hadn't imagined quite this scenario, but how perfect. I love Wisconsin sports! So did he. As I approached the stadium that day, I felt a comfort as if God was my escort. I knew God was with me, as He had always been. This longing in my heart will finally be filled. A deep desire only He knew.

I felt like a little girl again, wanting to please her father. I hoped Stan would like me. I imagined a future together which included more Brewers games!

We met after the first inning. I had to walk up from the lower level. How will I find him? I don't know what he looks like. Even with all the noise and people, I felt guided right to him. There he was at the top of the stairs. I knew it was Stan.

He was looking around with anticipation too. He wore a Brewers hat, and he had a grey beard, rosy cheeks and a grin on his face. "Stan?" I said smiling. He nodded. I gave him a quick hug.

I could see myself in him, immediately. We talked through the whole game. I don't even remember who won! We hung out the rest of the evening together until after midnight.

It was at that moment I realized, it was Easter Sunday.

Resurrection Sunday!

A day of celebration.

Not only did God orchestrate an amazing day but He topped it off by doing it Easter weekend; a day of forgiveness, reconciliation and rebirth!

I am so my father's daughter. All those things about me weren't a mystery any more. My life made sense! It was the beginning of a wonderful friendship; a beautiful father/daughter relationship. It was a miracle, and an answer to a prayer.

Hebrews 11:1 says, *Faith is the substance of things hoped for, the evidence of things not seen.* It was in total surrender. My faith through prayer over that post-it note that activated my miracle. In the spiritual realm, things were put in motion. I believed, and I received!

At Easter service, I poured my worship out to the Lord. I was so thankful for my miracles and answered prayers. It was in the pursuit of my birth mother and the longing to know my birth father that I recognized God's pursuit of me. God wanted me to see with my "spiritual eyes" that through Jesus, I can look like Him. I can act like Him. Because of Jesus, God sees me as perfect.

The revelation of the true miracle was recognizing I was adopted in God's family first. God loves me…with His perfect love. I'm one of His children and He wants a personal relationship with me.

I was supposed to be drawn closer to my heavenly father and drawn into relationship with Jesus.

God chose my biological father. He handpicked the father to raise me. No earthly person, no one I dated, not my parents who raised me, not my birth parents, could ever fulfill my heart's needs. It was God's love that made my heart whole. My heart is full, complete because of His love. My future together with Him was secured through Jesus.

It was the love of God, our Father in heaven that turned my brokenness and emptiness into something beautiful. A beautiful love story. HIS love story with me.

It can be your love story too.

Peggy Noonan:

"I think miracles exist in part as gifts and in part as clues that there is something beyond the flat world we see."

CANDICE

MOE

Candice Moe is a servant of God living in Trinidad. She no longer works as a flight attendant, but has had every need met by God as she draws nearer to Him.

Candice spreads the gospel to those around her and online through the sharing of scriptures and she studies the bible daily.

—— Chapter 13 ——

AMAZING GRACE: HOW SWEET A SOUND

Candice Moe

"I praise you because I am fearfully and wonderfully made; your works are wonderful, I know that full well."

~Psalm 139:14 (NIV)

I remember it as though it were yesterday.

I was standing in the school yard, as a young girl all of seven- or eight-years old, being belittled and ridiculed. I remember children saying that only my mother could ever love me because they thought my appearance so repulsive. Growing up I had a bad overbite and the other children just thought I looked awful. I remember feeling they were right and, little did I know, that experience would usher me into a life of low self-esteem and wanting to fit in.

Another of my earliest memories was that guys seemed to like me just fine. The children in my neighborhood were predominately male and I didn't feel ugly around them at all. As the years passed, my self-esteem remained at rock bottom, but most would never have known it. I put on a show, although I never consciously knew I was acting. I figured out quickly that guys liked me and girls seldom did. I started seeking approval from them and I craved the attention, though I'd never let on that I did.

My mother was born again when I was about nine and it was a supernatural experience...one that I witnessed. I distinctly recollect Jesus speaking through my mother and saying to me, "Candice you have a kind heart, but you're too disrespectful to your parents!"

While in primary school, I had gotten a wart on my finger and I used a pin in an effort to remove it. That bright idea ended up working in reverse and soon I had many warts to count. My parents bought every product available, but nothing worked. One day, as my mom was watching TBN, Marilyn Hickey said the Lord asked her to pray for people with skin conditions. My mom suggested that I put my hands on the TV and pray along, then she left the room.

I put my hands on the television and repeated a super short prayer. Afterwards, I went to find my mom and let her know what we'd prayed. She said to me, "Candice, look at your hands!" As I looked at my hands, my jaw hit the floor because every single wart, and—believe me—there were many, had disappeared!! Gone! Vanished into thin air; not even a scar or a shred of evidence was lingering behind.

I witnessed a lot of the supernatural growing up and I would always sense the presence of angelic and demonic beings. I was so aware of them that I was afraid to be alone, especially in the shower. That was the place the demonic spirits would attack me with fear the most. Even washing my face was something I seldom did since it meant having to close my eyes. Eventually, in my teens, I developed acne and would go on to suffer from it for many years. Imagine how that worked on my self-esteem! As an acne-laden teen without self-worth, my desperate yet covert need to feel loved and desired translated into self-defeating behaviors, a boat load of regret, and a series of failed and toxic relationships complete with abuses, rapes, and abortions.

Despite all that was bubbling inside, I actually managed to have a fairly normal childhood. My siblings and I weren't afforded the degree of freedom most kids seemed to enjoy. When we did get to go out with friends, we were dropped off and picked up by our parents. As I got further into my teenage years, this really started to infuriate me because through my eyes, everyone could have could fun but me.

When I was twenty-one, I was hired as a flight attendant and so began an outwardly fabulous life of travel an adventure. I love me some retail therapy and I've always been a giver, so Christmas time was my delight. I was the one with the big garbage bags full of gifts, so much so that my father often referred to me as Ms. Claus. I have been blessed to have had amazing vacations to places like Egypt, Spain, and France. Life was overtly envious but inside I was perishing. Because you're flying, your schedule is not in line with others. You're not able to be around in community with other people. We were acquaintances and friendly, but didn't really have time together. I had always wanted to feel included. Because I didn't have those close friendships early in life, I had a strong desire to not be alone.

The thing I truly desired was a committed relationship. I wanted someone to love me and someone I could love. When I was a child I would always say to myself that I only wanted one boyfriend and that he would become my husband. I was always in love with "love".

> *I wanted someone to love me and someone I could love.*

As the years progressed, however, my personal decisions became increasingly tumultuous. Desperate for love, or at least the appearance of it, I entered into relationships where I knew I was settling, enduring abuse, feeling unloved, unwanted, and disrespected. I'd date men I knew, in most cases, I would never marry but they fed my craving to hear I was beautiful and I was so hungry for affirmation, I completely threw caution (and good sense) to the wind and convinced myself, somewhat, that we loved each other. In reality, though, I was broken and so were they.

Everything changed in December 2010. Returning from a flight on ole years evening, I fell and sustained injuries that caused life as I knew it to abruptly end. As a crew, we approached the Customs Hall. I was first in line to have my luggage checked. As I made my way to the egress I suddenly felt myself falling. I got up, thankful that the airport was not heavily populated, warned the remaining crew members to avoid, what seemed like a bucket of water had been spilled and proceeded to the company transportation. Two days later, while operating another flight, I found myself in excruciating pain. I had been flying for over six years by then and I knew the pain was not normal. After several months on injury leave and later an MRI, it was discovered that there was a tear in the rotator cuff muscle and significant damage had occurred. As a flight attendant, there is mandatory annual training, safety drills, and other procedures for which you must be deemed physically fit-to-fly and job competent. Additionally, I had already begun pilot training. Aviation is a field I quite enjoyed for many years so being told by physicians that the usual recovery time for these injuries was three to four years and later finding out that surgery had been proposed, was a whole lot to take in.

I was told that the usual recovery for my injuries was three to four years. For the better part of the first year, I was forced to spend a lot of time lying down and—when you're down—you tend to look up. Increasingly, I would have this overwhelming urge to read the Bible. I would read the Bible for hours every day and, the more I read, the more insatiable my hunger for the Word became. Suddenly I realized how incredibly Loving JESUS is and that He'd Been pursuing me my entire life. I saw His hand on my Life and—equally as important—I finally saw my great need for a Savior! Before long, it was too strong to ignore and so I embarked on a journey through the Scriptures.

Initially, I asked the Lord if I would make it back to work. I remember him saying to me, 'If you want to go back, I'll let you, but I have something else in mind for you to do.'

I told the Lord, 'Okay. I'll lay down.'

Here I was, lying in bed, feeling without purpose as I was unable to work, not valuing myself, being with men who were abusive, and feeling miserable.

How was this me?

How was this what had become of MY life?

Bawling my lungs out, I confessed every single sin I could think of and begged the Father to save me from this mess of a life I'd created. "Jesus I've completely screwed up but if you can fix it and fix me, I surrender it all to You."

I was still with somebody because I couldn't be alone. I told the Lord, I'd rather have who was his choice. God told me that, even when I feel alone, I'm not lonely. I have Him.

> *I was still with somebody because I couldn't be alone.*

God causes us to go after HIM more.

From that moment to this, such Peace has engulfed me that there are no words that can adequately describe it to you. I can only admonish you to experience it yourself.

When I think back on life before Jesus, I feel such overwhelming gratitude! Gratitude that the God who had shown me His power from such a tender age, the God I had accepted into my heart as a young girl, but turned so very far from as a teenager and particularly as a young adult, never turned away from me. God stayed with me... Jesus stayed married to me (Jeremiah 3:14) even though I was so unfaithful to Him. Even though I was the vilest of sinners! What a mighty God we get to belong to! He is so incredibly full of compassion and mercy!

Since turning my life over to God, I've been filled with such joy and peace in getting to know and experience Abba's Love and

I've seen such miracles that I often say to myself, "Why did you wait so long?" I made a deal with Jesus that if He would help me spiritual mature quickly, teach me Himself everything I should know and make the Bible real to me, I would give Him unlimited ownership of my life. That proposition was a win-win for me, but I not so jokingly said to Jesus that He got the raw end of the stick having the task of refining me. Still, promptly, He assured me that He loves me from start to finish. I must confess, life in His hands is oh so amazingly awesome!

In reading the Bible one day, I saw that Jesus came to redeem me, not just from hell, but from missing out on every spiritual gift He had already lain out for me. All of a sudden, His revelation hit me that I don't have to put up with anything that came as a result of Adam's sin. Jesus' death, resurrection and ascension purchased for me an even better deal than Adam had. Every menstrual cycle for as long as I could remember, I would experience such painful cramps that without medication, it was difficult to function but now I had a not so secret weapon- the Living Word of God. I wasted no time. Immediately, putting my hands on my stomach, I asserted my authority over the spirit of pain and infirmity and commanded my body to fall in line with the Promises of Christ for the Word says, "By His stripes I AM healed!" Allow me to brag on our Jesus by testifying that I have not had even the slightest discomfort during my cycle since! This was the first of many Revelations Holy Spirit would teach me.

"By His stripes, I AM healed!"

Sid Roth has an investigative program called, "It's Supernatural!" He airs testimonies of people who move in the supernatural Power of God. This was intriguing to me because I had begun seeing into the spirit realm much more clearly and more frequently, since becoming a Christian. I'd been experiencing signs and wonders and I was led by Holy Spirit to watch episodes featuring people with prophetic gifts. The Father had been opening up to me the ministry of the prophetic and I was often being used by Abba to deliver prophetic messages to complete strangers. Each time his guest would speak a release of the anointing they carried over the audience, Holy Spirit would have me say, "I receive a double portion in JESUS Name."

There was one day in particular, I remember the Holy Spirit led me to watch hours and hours of prophetic teaching from specific people whose names He would give me. Later that evening, I went to church, where many of the leaders and members of the congregation are also prophetic. In my personal time with the Father that day, I had read in the :

"...stir up the gifts given to you by the laying on of hands." (Timothy 4:14 and 2 Timothy 1:6 NIV).

Paul's directive seemed to leap off the page at me and I inquired of the Holy Spirit, for if I was the one responsible for bringing out what the Father placed within me, I was desperate to know how to go about doing it. After service, I stayed back to encourage the elder who had preached letting him know that he had taught on the very topic Holy Spirit raised to me and answered the very question I had posed to the Lord earlier. The Holy Spirit had given me His answer through the mouth of His child, who is also prophetic. Indeed, I was to stir it up and the way to do it was by stepping out in faith, obeying the anointing of Holy Spirit to give His Word to whomever He would have me give it to. Imagine my delight in discovering I had been "stirring it up" all along. The elder then proceeded to tell me that Holy Spirit had identified me as a prophet of God and directed him to speak a prayer of release over me right then and there. I thanked him and went home rejoicing for I had just been given a Heavenly kiss.

With all this happening, there was still the issue of being on industrial injury leave for such a prolonged period. Months before the injury, I had taken a student loan, in addition to the auto loan already being deducted from my salary. Since I was not flying, I was only receiving my base salary and two loans were now being repaid from it. Subsequently, each month I was left with significantly less money than what I had grown accustomed to.

Prior to the accident, I'd been tithing fifteen percent, as, even in my horribly sinful state, I never neglected to tithe and to bless the church financially each month. By this time, my reliance on Jesus was being firmly established and He was confirming for me that He was and must always be my only Source of every supply. In obedience, I had given away all the money in my savings account and I was literally living paycheck to paycheck. By Abba's Grace, I was singular and immovable in my commitment to trust the Lord as my Provider. I resolved to tithe twenty percent and so, for over two years, I had an average of $200 a month. It was a drastic difference from what I enjoyed pre-injury, which often amounted in excess of $12,000 a month.

One day I asked the Father: "Please do something because this is just too constrictive, I can't go on like this. I know You're teaching me that I don't live by bread alone and You know I trust You, but this is just too much."

I still can't tell you what Jesus did but, the very next month, after my tithes and everything else that had been coming out of my salary were set aside, there remained $800! I was so excited! What Abba spoke next took every ounce of faith I had and tears began to fill my eyes. His voice was so calming as He replied, "Daughter, do you remember the house I showed you that's en route to church? I want you to give them the entire $800."

My stomach sank but my spirit, full of the Word of God, rose up within me and I said, "I'll do anything You ask because I trust You and I know You Love me." The timing couldn't have been worse. My cycle was coming, I was all out of toiletries, and I wasn't going to ask my parents for assistance.

The next time I went to church, I stopped at the house and gave them the total amount. Naturally, that was a very difficult month but my confidence was on full blast because I knew the Heart of my Father was not to take from me but to bless to me. When the following payday arrived, I set aside my tithes and offerings and began counting what I assumed would be $800. Instead, the Father had given me $1,600! My gratitude was exceedingly full, not merely for the finances, but because Jesus had granted me the opportunity to see that faith and obedience will always be rewarded. I had put a smile on the face of JESUS, Who is, not only my Lord, but also my Friend. It is forever cemented in my heart that my Papa God is Faithful!

> *I had put a smile on the face of Jesus....*

With God in my heart, no matter what relationships are in my life, I'm never alone. By allowing Him to be number one in my life, I was able to lay down my old life and find a new one in healing and prophetically sharing His Word. He meets my every need and uses me for His Glory.

It's amazing growing up in Christ! A life completely surrendered to Jesus really is life and life lived more abundantly.

From a horridly broken mess of a girl to a young woman who sees in the spirit realm, prophesies, sees the sick made well, and casts out demons.

I continue to experience such thrilling adventures living for Christ, but–by leaps and bounds—my absolute favorite came on Friday the 13th of February in 2015. Reading the Bible and seeing how Jesus had appeared to so many, my heart's desire became to see Him face-to-face. Then, finally, in the early hours of that beautiful Friday morning, the Lord of Glory appeared to me! I had just awoken from a dream where Jesus and I were reaching the lost with the Gospel and, no sooner had I opened my eyes, than I knew my life would never be the same!

By this time in my life, seeing angels was a common occurrence, but I knew this morning was unlike any other. Waking up lying on my left side, I could sense His presence to my right but—in attempting to turn around—I realized I could do nothing more than blink my eyes. His Presence, His Glory was so strong that my mortal body couldn't bear it. I cried out to the Father to please give me the strength and immediately my neck was loosed and I was able to move my head, although the rest of my body remained immobilized. There simply are no words to describe the collage of emotions that I felt when my eyes met my Savior, my Lord, my Husband (Ephesians 5:25-27 NIV), my Best Friend!

For me in this moment, He was wearing, what I can only liken to a very sheer curtain of brilliant Light. It enveloped Him and without saying an audible word, Jesus spoke to my spirit telling me He had dimmed His Glory to enable the movement of my head. He remained long enough for me to see His features, and then He slowly faded away.

As He slipped back into the spiritual realm, my mobility returned and I shouted out, "You came, I knew You would come! I can no longer see You but I know You're still here!"

To this day, no miracle or wonder has topped that experience. Acts 26:16 (NLT) had never been more real to me: *"Now get to your feet! For I have appeared to you to appoint you as My servant and witness. Tell people that you have seen Me, and tell them what I will show you in the future."*

Recently, I found an old photo of my teenaged self. With an ear to ear smile I said, "Wait until you see what Jesus will do in your life!" I knew when I looked at that picture that in HIS eyes, she had always been beautiful.

Dwight Longenecker:

"Maybe miracles are given not to prove anything, but simply to remind us that the physical world is not so solid and real and dependable as we think."

CINDY

CHRISTOFFERSON

Cindy Christofferson is the Senior Pastor of RockWood Church in Waukesha, Wisconsin. While asked to write her story of becoming a pastor, she is grateful to share this God inspired journey. She believes readers will truly see God as a personal God, who speaks to, equips us, and directs all of His people. When we follow God, hold on because He will take us places we never dreamed imaginable. Cindy resides in Waukesha with her husband Donny. They have three grown children and seven grandchildren. She enjoys spending time with her family and relaxing on the beach admiring God's beautiful creation. For more information, please visit: www.RockWoodChurch.net or connect with Cindy at: Cindy@RockWoodChurch.net.

——Chapter 14——

PUZZLE PIECES

Cindy Christofferson

"(Be) confident of this, that he who began a good work in you will carry it on to completion until the day of Christ Jesus."

ॐ Philippians 4:6 (NIV)

If you were to ask me who my hero was when I was a little girl I would have to say Joseph. You may be wondering, Joseph who? Are you familiar with the story of Joseph in the Old Testament? That Joseph.

God gave Joseph prophetic dreams. He was favored by his father, hated and sold into slavery by his brothers, falsely accused, imprisoned and was still faithful to God. During his time in prison,

God gave Joseph interpretations of dreams and he went from prison to the palace in a day.

Each of those events was part of a bigger picture God had prepared for him before the foundations of the earth; puzzle pieces that were crafted by the very own hands of God. You see, his story is no different than ours, full of puzzle pieces that God, Himself created and He is putting together your story for His glory.

Little Catholic Girl

Sometimes miracles are instantaneous. Those are awesome. I questioned God many times and asked Him why I was the only girl in my family. There wasn't much chance of my playing with dolls as I was brought up with four brothers; two older and two younger. You'd often see me playing some kind of sport with "the boys." It's who I was, and how God created me to be; a little tomboy. Oh…but I would have to put my makeup on and fix my hair before I jumped onto the basketball court.

I knew the voice of God at a young age. In fact, the Holy Spirit was my best friend. I didn't tell people I talked to God and He talked back to me. I honestly thought they'd put me in a straitjacket and send me to an insane asylum.

As a little Catholic girl, I loved to read about the saints. I never prayed to them; I just loved their devotion to Jesus. I was especially fond of Saint Joan of Arc. When I would read her story, my spirit would leap. She listened to the voice of God, and she led men into victory. I looked at her as a "Fighter for Christ." When I was in middle school, I made a promise to God that some day when I had a baby girl, I would name her after Saint Joan of Arc. Our second child was a girl, and we named her Jennifer JOAN.

My daughter was reminded frequently whom she was named after and that she was a "Fighter for Christ!" **Fast forward twenty some years, during a service, I heard the Lord tell me so clearly that I was** *the Joan of Arc.* I was quite surprised. What did He mean? I didn't know but I did know the voice of God.

Put Me In, Coach!

"You want me to what? You want me to coach boy's baseball? But I'm a girl!" I said confused. Our son D.J.'s friends wanted to play on the same baseball team together and the only way they were guaranteed to be on the same team was if they would supply a coach. No fathers were able to commit to the job or had the desire to coach. "We'll support you!" said the parents of the boys. And that they did.

We started playing baseball in a nearby town. I coached the boys' baseball team, and it was an amazing experience. It was time for us to move the team to our hometown, which also happened to be the top athletic school district in the state.

They were not ready for a woman to be the head coach of a boy's baseball team. And since we had the team and a coach, there was nothing they could do about it. It never even crossed my mind it would be a problem. But, it sure was. "A woman coaching boy's baseball?!" The gossip started flying. "She's just a woman trying to prove something in a man's world!" Finger pointing and rude comments appeared to be the norm; even at the local grocery store. "Hey, there's that woman!" I would hear. For two years, the rumors kept flying as I kept on doing what I was called to, and that was coach. Yet, I did not say a word. I kept silent.

Finally; a break. The heads of the league no longer saw me as that woman trying to prove something in a man's world, but someone called to coach. They started to respect me and even asked me to be their first female Baseball Commissioner. I was honored to take on that role.

I ended up coaching for nearly two decades. Not only did I coach boys' baseball, but boys' basketball, as well as girls' basketball and softball.

I obviously did not realize it at that time but *God was preparing and equipping me* for such an incredibly challenging position that was years in front of me. The position was a Woman Senior Pastor. Pastoring is a lot like coaching. I see each believer as part of "God's Team," and on God's Team there is an unlimited amount of players who can get onto the playing field. God doesn't want bench warmers or you could say, pew sitters. God wants His children to use their gifts, to fulfill their own story; their own playbook. Or you could say, God wants them to get into the game. And as you probably know, a Woman Senior Pastor isn't the norm so you can only imagine the amount of persecution that goes along with that position.

The Prophetic

The Lord moved my husband, Donny and I to a newer church plant called Family Chapel. (The name was changed to RockWood when we purchased a building). We knew we were called there, yet at that time the Lord's plans didn't speak to me as to why. Two years in the church and complete silence. I didn't understand God's plan for me. There were many times I cried and at times sobbed. "Why God?! I have a fire and zeal for you! I could be used in the churches in Milwaukee! Can I please leave?!" Silence. All I wanted to do was perhaps lead a Small Group! Something, anything. I remember texting James, the Lead Pastor and asking him if I could clean the church for free. No response. I thought, *'Lord, I can't even clean the toilets here!'*

After crying out to God for what seemed like the thousandth time, the Lord gave me a vision. In the vision I saw a rushing river. There were stepping stones placed in a pathway across the river. I knew the stepping stones represented my life, and once I crossed the river, my life would come to completion. I felt the Lord was telling me I needed to focus only on the stepping stone He had me on right now. He would move me to the next stepping stone in His time. That vision gave me God's supernatural peace to wait and continue to trust in God's perfect plan for my life.

I wasn't very familiar with the prophetic. I knew it was biblical; however, I had my reservations. A prophet named Tom Stamman came to our church. He gave me a word that I would be a reverend and would see me preach some day. He probably saw me roll my eyes. Being a pastor was never, even on my radar. Not once, in my life had I ever desired or even thought of being a pastor. In fact, I didn't really believe in women pastors.

At that time I was attending Midwest Bible College. It wasn't something I shared with many people. I felt lead to go to this college for spiritual growth and discipline. My friends who knew I was attending kept telling me I was going to be a pastor. I responded, "Whatever!" Again...not on my radar!

Years had passed and Tom was in town again ministering at a different church. Tom prays over thousands of people each year. He had no clue who I was. I told him what church I had attended. He knew James, our Lead Pastor, and the fact we had lost five pastors in a six month period. It was almost humorous. And that is when Tom gave me a prophetic word and said, "You are the one who James has been praying for." He continued to prophesy. The prophecy was recorded and I wrote it down and saved it in my back pocket. Not knowing exactly what it meant.

Being called into the Lead Pastor's office was just as scary as being called into the principal's office. As I sat there, I could feel my heart pound through my chest. My pulse felt like it was going a million miles a second. We sat there and started to have a general conversation when I heard the voice of God so clearly, "He is going to raise you above the rest!" What…no way?! I thought to myself.

We continued our conversation and about twenty minutes later James dropped the bomb and said, "Well, if I'm going to be a fool, I'll be a fool for Christ. Would you possibly be interested in being our Executive Pastor?" I knew it was God. The problem was I had NO idea who an Executive Pastor was. James gave me a briefing, but the first thing I did when I got into my car was Google…*What is an Executive Pastor?*

The following day I read James the prophetic word that was given to me by Tom months earlier.

I became RockWood's Executive Pastor.

Dreams…Warning Of The Battles Ahead

Nearly two years had passed and James had starting talking to the board about possibly leaving his position as Lead Pastor.

James, along with his wife, Cheri faithfully started the church in their living room almost seven years earlier, and now he wasn't sure what the future held. My husband and I really wanted them to stay. James was not only our pastor, he and his wife became our friends.

The Lord speaks to people in numerous ways.

The Lord speaks to people in numerous ways. This time God spoke to me through a dream. In fact, I had two dreams that evening. In the first dream, I was driving a car with only one hand on the steering wheel. A car quickly dashed out in from of me; I slammed on my breaks and just missed hitting the car. I started to proceed when another car dashed out in front of me. Again, I slammed on my breaks just missing yet another car. I put both hands on the steering wheel and held on tight. As I accelerated again, I approached a railroad crossing. The arm was up and just as I was about to cross, a train appeared out of nowhere. I missed hitting the train, and then I woke up.

I knew the Lord was showing me there were going to be attacks against me one after the other with next to no time in between. The second dream was regarding James. I woke up and knew he would resign.

We continued to work behind the scenes if James decided to resign. One of the options would mean that I would lose my position, solely because I was a woman. It was disheartening. I knew I had to give it over to the Lord. I chose to stay silent. The Lord gave me a verse that I stood on, He said that *He would fight for me, and I shall hold my peace.* Exodus 14:14. I would see this verse or hear this verse wherever I went. A friend of mine not knowing what was going on came into my office one day and brought me a gift. She told me the Lord told me to give this to you. It was a decorative plate with an easel and you guessed it, yes,

Exodus 14:14. I knew the Lord would fight for me, and I was to hold my peace.

Didn't See That Coming

The morning of January 6th, 2015 I had another dream. In my dream, I was at a football game, alone in the stands, but the bleachers were crowded...completely packed. It was a nice fall night that didn't even leave need for a jacket. The football field didn't look familiar, but, in your dreams, you know where places are and I believed it was in Waukesha...the very city where my puzzle would soon start coming together. I looked at the scoreboard and the clock read two seconds. One of the teams was about to kick a field goal for the win when something unexpected happened. In the middle of this beautiful night, a downpour of rain and hail began. Everyone, including myself, started running for cover. It seemed like I was the only one going toward the concession stand; everyone else was going under the bleachers. I didn't feel cold or wet. I just ran as fast as I could toward the end zone and what looked like a concession stand. And because of all the hail, a massive fire was blazing in the end zone...the hail was causing flames. It was almost like, instead of rain and hail, it was fire and brimstone. It looked like a glimpse of hell.

I entered what looked like a concession stand. A young man came inside with me. I perceived him to be my youngest son Jesse, yet it didn't look like him. The building started to elevate. As it was elevating a man came into the shelter. The man glared at me with evil in his eyes. I perceived him to be Satan. He walked towards me. I was afraid, but I felt a boldness. I put my arm out and blocked the young man, like when you have to stop a car quickly and protect the person sitting next to you. I reached into a drawer that was to my right and grabbed a large knife. He continued to come toward me and glared into my eyes. I then forcefully stabbed him in the heart. He heartlessly looked at me and laughed. I then quickly pulled out the knife, and immediately stabbed him in the head, and then abruptly woke up questioning...what was that all about?!

Just an FYI...Disclaimer - I've never had a dream about stabbing a person but Satan had appeared in a dream of mine years earlier. And James gave me the interpretation of that dream that a promotion was coming.

Without his knowledge of the dream I had earlier that morning, then that same evening James emailed his resignation letter to me as well as the rest of the board. That letter stated I would be the Senior Pastor of RockWood Church starting February 1st, 2015. I was in shock.

Looking back I knew God had been preparing me. Scared? Heck yeah! Why would You put me in this position God? Doubt and disbelief? You betcha! Again, I knew it was God.

Confirmations

I was asked to teach at a prayer meeting. There were about forty people in attendance. I only knew a handful of them, and I was extremely nervous because I didn't like talking in front of people. It was a Friday evening and in just two days James would be announcing his resignation as well as inform the church that I would be their new Senior Pastor. God does have a sense of humor; putting someone in the position of Senior Pastor who does not like public speaking.

The host introduced me as the Executive Pastor of RockWood Church. With a lump in my throat, I brought forth the message the Lord had put in my heart. As I was preparing to leave, a man whom I had never met before told me he had a word from the Lord for me. His name was Daniel.

He said that the Lord is promoting you. You are anointed. You will not know what to do, but it will be like cross-stitch. And he moved his hand like he was cross-stitching, just one stitch at a time. I don't think I could have opened my eyes any wider. I was shocked and overjoyed at the same time. He had NO idea what was going to be announced on Sunday. I asked him if he could share this word with my husband, Donny and my friend, Carmen who were in the other room. They were blown away as well. We all knew that was a word from the Lord.

A short time later I found out a little more about Daniel and how he defended me and the position God had given me even though he went to another church which did not allow women to pastor or preach. I was overwhelmed by God's goodness in sending someone to give me a word. He knew I would need it.

After about nine months as the Senior Pastor, I cried out to God for the umpteenth time. *"Are you sure God?! Is this where I'm supposed to be? You know there are many other people out there that can do this job better than me?"* I heard the Lord say, "Look up Joan of Arc's birthday." Thank God for Google. I looked up Joan of Arc's birthday, and it was January 6th. That's the same day I had the dream that I was staring down at Satan, and that's the same day James resigned and that I found out I was going to be the Senior Pastor of RockWood Church.

God is so gracious and merciful. He is so faithful. He is so patient. And when we cry out to Him, He is there to encourage and strengthen us. Like He did when I cried out to Him again after being the Senior Pastor for well over a year. "Okay God, I keep putting down fleeces because I do not want to be outside Your will for my life! I need to know that I am where I am supposed to be! You have to show me God. I want You to show me something relating to MY name, not Joan of Arc, my name, seven years ago when I first starting coming to this church. Something that I would know that I know Lord!" A seemingly impossible cry out to God.

We wanted to do an outreach at a local farmer's market and since we were a nonprofit we could get a space for free. Mark, one of our congregants, who loved Jesus and RockWood, was applying for our "free space" and called me to ask for our tax exempt status form (501c3 form). I have seen that form dozens of times over the years and noticed something that day I had never noticed before. Our church started over eight years earlier, but the process of becoming 501c3 status can take a long time. The tax exempt status form showed the date the church legally became established. **The official date of RockWood Church aka Family Chapel, Inc. being established was April 20th, 2009. My birthday; seven years ago.**

Earlier that day, I had cried out to God and asked Him to show me something…anything that I would know from seven years ago that had my name on it and not Joan of Arcs. I needed to know this was God's will for my life. God was faithful to that fleece that I laid down. I knew that I knew that I knew it was where God wanted me to be.

He continues to show His amazing grace to me. I was crying out to God…again early one Tuesday morning! I felt like I kept messing up and that He should take me out of this position. "God…give me a sign today! I want a sign today regarding

RockWood! Give me a sign that I know I am STILL supposed to be the Senior Pastor here! If not God, I will go!"

I don't know how long the Lord will have me in this position. It could be another day, year or decade. That's up to God. This is what I do know, my identity isn't in my position, but my identity is who I am in Christ.

A few hours later, I went to RockWood Church and saw the sign. This time was an actual, literal sign. We purchased the building over four years earlier but never had the money for a sign. We had a banner with our name on it; sandwich boards. We also had RockWood on the illuminated rolling sign, but no actual sign. I knew we had ordered a sign. I had no idea they were going to surprise me with it. Norm, a faithful servant of God, insisted that sign had to go up that Monday evening. Mark and his wife, Val didn't understand why because it was going to have to go down right away to work on the electrical components of the sign, but Norm insisted. Norm had no idea, but God did. He knew I would be crying out to Him and needed "a sign." As I approached RockWood, I looked up and tears started rolling down my face. I was overwhelmed by God's goodness. He gave me that sign. That's my God!

These are just a few of the many pieces of my puzzle...of my story that will someday come to completion once I cross over the river. The Lord is putting your puzzle together; your story as well. He will move you to your next stepping stone. *You are to trust in the Lord with all your heart, and lean not on your own understanding, acknowledge Him, and HE will direct your paths.* (Proverbs 3:5-6)

Robert H. Schuller:

"Impossible situations can become possible miracles."

MARY KAY
SWITTEL

Mary Kay Swittel is passionate about telling her story of perseverance. She is an avid learner of mindfulness, self-healing and nutrition. She is always looking for ways to improve her personal, mental and spiritual life. She has boundless energy and is always challenging improvement in herself, her family, and her business. Mary Kay resides in Greendale, Wisconsin with her husband Gary and children Sydnie and Sam. She is a Packer season ticket holder, Brewer fan and loves traveling with her family, mountain biking, kayaking, road riding with her Mom Millie, reading, and walking her dog, Jameson. To reach Mary Kay, please visit www.facebook.com/mkswittel or e-mail mk@swittel.com.

—— Chapter 15 ——

WHEN LIFE GIVES YOU LYME...FIND YOUR LEMONS!

Mary Kay Swittel

"You were given this life because you are strong enough to live it!"

ဆ *Unknown*

*T*his quote by an anonymous author is my mantra and engraved on a bracelet that was gifted to me at a special time of my healing journey. Life is truly a gift and I choose to BELIEVE! I thank God every single day for blessing me with Lyme Disease. Yes; you heard it correctly; I thank God every day for Lyme, a disease which has changed my life and the lives of my loved ones forever. My appreciation for my illness did not happen immediately. It happened as God began placing amazing people in front of me at the perfect moment in time.

Have you ever been completely lost?

There was a time when I was so sick and painfully ill, that I didn't want to be alive. I could not sleep or think straight and I felt anxious and depressed. I was lost and didn't have the inner strength to move forward on my own. I needed to go deeper

> *I was so sick and painfully ill that I didn't want to be alive.*

within myself and ask for God's help and direction. It was time for prayer and deep compassion...for myself. I found it difficult to love myself when I had zero motivation to get through each and every day.

I remember a cool, damp, dreary, March day in 2013. I visited Father Matthew Widder at St. Mary Parish. I knew I needed that strength. At that moment in time, I was pretty low. He was one of the first people I sought other than family. He had a foundational spirituality that I needed at the time. It was always hard for me to reach out beyond my close-knit circle, but I felt called to reach out to him. He was a man I completely trusted, even though trust was never one of my strong traits. Trust had always been something which needed extra building in any relationship I had. Something about Father Matthew and the words he spoke at mass gave me the strength to trust and share my desperate need for his spirituality in my healing. God allowed this trust to grow so His message could be shared.

Father Matthew met with me, listened to me, and prayed for me. We exchanged laughs and tears but I recall these specific words I will never forget:

"God does not want you to suffer…EVER!"

I left the church thinking and feeling like something just clicked. Something felt empowering. For the next thirty to forty-five days, all day, every day, those words would constantly come to my mind.

A-ha!

The light bulb went on…this became my miracle moment; Father Matthew's simple words of compassion gave me the strength to consciously decide I was NEVER going to give up. The Father opened my eyes and my

> *I had the desire, compassion, belief, and determination to begin loving myself again.*

heart to actively *begin* healing. When my heart healed, I had the strength to deal with what I thought might never heal…my Lyme Disease.

I had the desire, compassion, belief, and determination to begin loving myself again. Knowing God did not want me to suffer was exactly what I needed to hear at that very moment. The road would be long, but I had this incredible Miracle to focus on moving forward. Nothing would stand in my way as I began the road to healing.

"He has perfect timing: never early, never late. God is never in a hurry, but he is always on time." (Peter 3:8 NIV)

My life was pretty ordinary before I fell sick with Lyme Disease. I am the wife of a man who is the most positive human being I know. Gary was and still is my ROCK, best friend, love of my life, and business partner. We have owned a successful, residential, real estate business for twenty-four years. It has been the perfect business for us while raising and participating in our children's lives. Sydnie and Sam work hard in school and have achieved terrific grades. They both play sports and are athletic and passionate, especially in baseball, softball, and volleyball. There is nothing better than watching your kids play and compete in the sports they love.

Gary and I have always been avid sports fans, so it was easy for us to make sure we attended each and every one of our kids' events. I was a mountain biker who enjoyed racing across the state of Wisconsin and even into the Upper Peninsula of Michigan. Being in the woods on my bike made me feel resilient, content, and powerful. I was finishing in the top ten in my age group consistently. Here I was, a suburban mother proudly living life in a way I thought was perfectly healthy and normal. I was the "laid back" one with everything going for me. Friends called on me for help and I was the first to say "yes." The school called me to volunteer and I felt obligated. The busier I was, the more content I would be. I felt happy when I was surrounded by people and dreaded being alone or having quiet time. "YES" was my favorite and most used word!

As I look back, in reality, I was in very bad shape. My "bucket" was slowly overflowing right before my eyes. The "bucket" I am referring to is explained best by my doctor/nutrition coach, Dr. Jay Davidson. The bucket theory states that you were born with a certain size bucket. Not everyone is born into an ideal situation. Likewise, our buckets keep getting filled as we live our lives. We all are exposed to chemicals, toxins, stress, death, pesticides, vaccines, amalgam fillings, pharmaceuticals and more. These things fill your bucket. The key to understanding this bucket theory is to know that symptoms and chronic inflammation kick in when the bucket is overflowing. Stress adds to the problem (adds to the bucket!) and it becomes a self-perpetuating downward spiral once it starts. Symptoms lead to more stress and you become sick. Sickness can appear as cancer for some, depression, or—in my case—an autoimmune disease called CLD – Chronic Lyme Disease. It was like Niagara Falls was cascading over the bucket with a vengeance. No one could recognize who I was, not even myself.

I grew up in a white-collar household with a father who worked hard and travelled often. My Mom stayed home with my brother and me. She kept us grounded! My brother landed in the hospital when I was in second grade; he was in third grade. We were tight siblings and "Irish Twins" at that. He was given penicillin and had an allergic reaction that took weeks of healing in Children's Hospital. As a child and a sister, I vividly remember this part of my life as worrisome and stressful. My teacher would pray for him as part of our morning prayer in the catholic classroom and I would cry. The sadness was unbearable at times as my Mom, Dad, and even my brother's doctors feared for his life.

My bucket began to fill.

By the time I was in high school, my parents decided life together was just not going to work. Not only was stress and peer pressure part of being a freshman, but also adding divorce put me in a fragile state of mind. I tried to stay strong and I turned to my friends and even inward to hold myself up and get through. I remember our pastor from church coming to the house to talk to my brother and me. I understood the compassion Father Straub was trying to convey through his deep spirit in Jesus Christ. He wanted us to turn to God and pray for guidance. My brother shut down and I was not having much of this advice at my age. I felt I could be strong and get through it on my own.

The bucket continued to fill.

Moving out of the house and off to college brought bouts of insomnia as I struggled with my new independence. Feeling homesick and not having a clear idea of what I wanted to study continued to be a stress point in my life. Growing up was happening faster than I ever imagined it could. Changing majors a few times was not part of my plan, but needed to be done to keep the sanity. Phone calls home to Mom, sometimes at 3:00 A.M., were what got me through this challenging four years of my life. By the grace of God I graduated with a Bachelor of Business Degree, but still had no idea how to move forward.

Life continued to add to my bucket.

In 2007, Gary and I were skiing in Colorado. I remember the moment when I looked at my right calf and discovered a tiny black mole with a jagged edge. I knew immediately in my heart that something was not right. My doctor thought it was nothing to worry about, but I insisted we

I knew immediately in my heart that something was not right.

get it checked out. Results came a few days later. It was melanoma caught at its earliest stage.

I had CANCER!

The dreaded word and the start of a battle I would not lose. My steadfast husband kept me positive and held me strong. I underwent surgery and gained a scar that serves as a forever reminder of a stressful time when my bucket continued to fill. Looking back, I believe God put this Cancer in my life as a sign and a wake-up call, but the timing was just not quite right. It was going to take more time for me to find the presence of Jesus Christ in my everyday life. My bucket overflowed when my daughter entered her middle school and high school years. Girls in their teenage years can be unkind and, sometimes, downright mean. The trauma of stress can affect your health in many different ways and my stress peaked; my bucket overflowed. I deeply believe, with my whole being, tick bite or not, I was going to become sick in some way or fashion. I am grateful Lyme Disease was put in my life and for the many lemons placed perfectly in my personal journey of health which were about to follow.

"He who has a WHY to live for can bear almost any HOW."

Gary, Sydnie and Sam were my WHY! I could do this.

Lyme Disease is caused by a spirochete - a corkscrew shaped bacterium called Borrelia burgdorferi. Lyme is called "The Great Imitator," because its symptoms mimic many other diseases. It can affect any organ in the body, including the brain and nervous system, muscles, joints, and even the heart. It is transmitted through the bite of a tick which has preyed on other animals such as a deer or a mouse. A first symptom for some is a bull's-eye rash.

Not me! Because I did not get an early diagnosis from the many, many doctors I saw, my Lyme Disease became chronic. The journey to find the true cause of my symptoms (and ultimately a Lyme diagnosis) took close to seven years!

"Trust in the Lord with all your heart, and do not rely on your own understanding. Acknowledge him in all your ways, and he will make your paths straight." (Proverbs 3:5 NIV)

My very first symptom was an unbalanced feeling when I walked. It was not vertigo or dizziness, just a feeling of being unstable. I could ride my bike or drive and not have this feeling. Walking at times was scary, to the point where I would have to sit down to gain composure. My ENT was the very first doctor visit I had. Doctor visit after doctor visit became my life for several years. Each and every doctor I saw was quick to write a prescription for a drug to make me feel better. I swear I could have filled my entire kitchen pantry with prescription medicines including Valium, anti-depressants, anti-anxiety meds, sleeping pills, medicine for constipation, pain medication for joints, and the list goes on and on. I was diagnosed with Meniere's Disease, constipation, fibromyalgia, depression/anxiety, and TMJ to name a few. My trust in doctors and western medicine was diminishing fast.

This is where I cannot thank my husband and my mom enough. These two lemons kept me focused and on track at all times. They said no to prescription medications when I could not. Each time I would take a pill it made me feel worse. I was desperate to try anything to make myself feel better. I thought the countless doctors and pills could fix me.

The deepest, darkest days came in late Autumn of 2012. Life was downright ugly and, to this day, I do not know how I found the strength to get through each and every dreary day. I did not sleep literally for close to ninety days. Not a wink! These are the days that are hard for me to think about even today.

My husband and I tried everything to get me to sleep. I took Ambien®, which made me crazy; it didn't make me sleep so much as it made me shudder. It didn't relax me at all; quite the opposite. I'd "wake up" and my kids would ask if I slept. Day after day after day. It was awful. I couldn't relax at night. I would close my eyes, but never really sleep. I remember that I felt guilty for keeping my husband up, so we actually went shopping for a twin bed. We put it up in the basement. (It didn't work.) I remember flopping on different beds throughout the house – I was Goldilocks. Too hard, too soft, too awake.

During this time of insomnia my ears also started ringing. The ringing of Tinnitus at times was a piercing hiss and sometimes a painful roar. Loud noises made me cringe. My anxiety grew to a level in which I could not enter a mall or grocery store where there were crowds of people and/or a lot of activity. I would panic and have to leave immediately. There was one afternoon in particular, just after Thanksgiving, at the lakefront in Shorewood Wisconsin at Atwater Beach where I honestly thought my life was too complicated to live for. In a daze, teeth chattering, looking out over Lake Michigan, I desperately pulled my cell phone out of my many layers of clothing and called my husband and then my mom. The two people I trusted would listen and help me get up off the frigid cold concrete pier and move forward with my life. God was definitely present in this moment.

God was definitely present in this moment.

Part of my journey to healing was spent in the city of Marlton, New Jersey. I was referred to a specialist for my TMJ. My jaw was incredibly painful and tight all the time. I knew I clenched and grinded my teeth at night just by the way I would wake up in the morning. Dr. Ira Adler diagnosed and treated me for my TMJ for 13 months. This commitment strengthened my bond with my husband immensely. One weekend per month we drove to the East coast for an adjustment to the orthotic I wore in my mouth. This mouthpiece shifted my jaw and kept me from clenching and grinding at night. Gary and I would wake in the deep dark hours of an early Saturday morning to drive 13 ½ hours straight through to Marlton, a city just across the Delaware River outside of Philadelphia. We would arrive in time for dinner and a restful night of sleep. My appointments were almost always first thing Monday morning. Immediately after the consult and adjustment with Dr. Adler we would get back on the road and drive straight home! When I think back to this part of my journey I think about the sacrifice my husband made to be at my side always keeping me positive and focused on the goal of healing. TMJ was eventually determined to be a symptom of Lyme. I do believe these trips were necessary in my healing and made Gary and my relationship stronger than ever.

Rebecca Keith was the first NP to tell me I had Lyme Disease without a positive test result. At my first appointment with Rebecca, who was located just north of Hayward Wisconsin, she told me she knew I had Lyme. She shared with me the reality of this disease in Wisconsin. She ordered a blood test called the Western Blot and the results came back neither positive or negative. This is quite common in Lyme patients~ which is why doctors don't know exactly how to test or treat people like me when I enter their office with so many crazy symptoms. Rebecca had me on a rotating prescription medication regimen for a little over 1 year. This grueling and expensive regimen did help in some ways but tore away at my digestive system wreaking havoc. Many symptoms were helped but my gut was left destroyed. This is the journey for me and Lyme.

My neighbor and dear friend Gerry Murphy was the next timely person God placed perfectly in front of me. My very Irish neighbor, a man who would drop everything to help me or anyone out, is a true lemon in my life. He is a perfect neighbor! It is what Gerry did at the opportune time that started abundant healing. I can never be thankful enough for his act of kindness. He presented me with a gift for taking care of his new puppy while he and his family were not home during the day. Things happen for a reason! Gerry bought me a book written by his chiropractor that would change my life forever. I read the book in two days and was left speechless. I contacted the author, Dr. Jay Davidson and after an interview and review of my medical records he agreed to be my coach. By simply listening to me, hearing my symptoms and what I had gone through, he knew to test me for Lyme and Heavy Metal Toxicity. My Lyme test results were finally positive and my mercury level was sky-high. Dr. Jay explained that by simply changing my lifestyle by eating right, taking supplements to re-build my immune system, detoxing heavy metals out of the body, getting the mercury filled cavities removed, and most importantly spiritually connecting and loving myself, it was possible to heal. From this point forward we were not looking at the past but instead taking 1 day at a time, being grateful, connecting with God and having compassion for myself and my life. What a gift God has given me! Dr. Jay has become my nutrition coach, my life coach, my doctor and a dear friend. My eyes and my heart were now ready to open and heal. What a miracle life itself is!

I believe you are what you eat. Nutritional changes made me feel better INSTANTLY. Consuming the right foods has been a Miracle in my healing process. My new diet eliminated all foods that cause inflammation. No more gluten and very few carbs in general, no more white sugar or dairy. The western diet is wreaking havoc on the health of our country and my eyes are open to this now more than ever. My family eats what I make and I have seen firsthand how you become what you eat. My son's eczema has disappeared and my husband and daughter have lost weight and feel strong. At age 50, Gary feels better than he has his entire life. No more bloating for me! I feel strong and focused because of what I eat. What a simple concept… I am having more fun with new recipes, tasty ingredients, spices and flavors! We eat organic fruits and vegetables and grass-fed meats to nourish the body. Yes, I do cheat on occasion. If I am going to a birthday party I will probably indulge in a piece of cake and a scoop of ice cream, however, I do know I feel better if I stick to the foods I know aren't damaging my body. The food our society is eating is the cause of many diseases like Diabetes, Parkinson's, Arthritis, thyroid issues and more. Through what I have learned about food and nutrition, I hope to continue to share my knowledge with others. Food is a big key to healing and being healthy!

Kimberly Krueger is my most recent lemon. This woman has already taught me how to trust God more deeply for the journey that lies ahead. She has taught me a deeper faith necessary for complete healing. I am reading the Bible and using God's words to heal. Yes, the diet and the lifestyle changes were necessary to heal. Finding God was even more important. Giving all glory to God is what Kimberly is instilling within me. Her words resonate with me! The miracle above all miracles is to trust God and everything he lays before me, to follow the path he is leading me on and to fully trust in him. She was the missing link in my journey. Kimberly is my spiritual teacher!

Today I continue my personal journey of healing. I wake up grateful to be alive and thank God for every day. I have a morning ritual of prayer, deep breathing, and yoga to keep me grounded. My bedtime ritual is journaling. I write about my day and include at least five or six things for which I am grateful. God continues to be my guiding light and inner strength and I trust him with my entire being. I affiliate God with "guide," today. I find and speak with God mostly in nature because this is where I am most content. While I am riding in the woods or hiking with my dog I ask God for healing and he gives me the strength to move on.

Compassion for others dealing with Lyme Disease is an important key to my future healing process. I have met many people struggling with this challenging and debilitating disease. Within this past year I met a neighbor, Kim, who is now a dear friend and fellow "Lymie". She contacted me in desperation after she received my information and story from her sister-in-law, who happens to be in my neighborhood Bunco group. I have learned from Kim that we each have our own paths of healing and strength in numbers is more powerful than anything. Kim's strength is giving me more fighting power as I move forward in my own healing. Her friendship is unique because we have so much in common. Being able to bounce things off of one another in our struggles is what I cherish the most.

The Lyme community is growing incredibly fast here in our beautiful forest-filled state of Wisconsin. I get phone calls from people often, who have received my name from someone else who knows my story. How amazing is that? I am open to helping others heal while sharing what I know and believe to be true from my own healing process. Sharing my story of strength is my goal in the hopes of helping as many people heal as I can. I want to give people hope and the strength they need to heal. HOPE is sometimes all someone needs to survive. Just by seeing me and how far I have come, shows these people they too can heal! God already has my days planned, I just continue to ask for his direction.

"So do not fear, for I am with you; do not be dismayed for I am your God. I will strengthen you and help you; I will uphold you with my righteous right hand." ~Isaiah 41:10

Over the course of my Lyme experience, I've heard bits of wisdom from doctors, other Lymies, friends, supporters and others. These belief statements of sort have become a mantra that I've posted. *They are more lemons in the midst of Lyme:*

o   I Believe we have not come this far to fail or give up now.
o   I Believe we are meant to go through storms before we see the beautiful sun.
o   I Believe the kingdom we live in is unshakable.
o   I Believe family become friends and friends become family.
o   I Believe all my hard work will pay off.
o   I Believe I have the power to change anything I do not like.
o   I Believe collectively we are stronger than we are apart.
o   I Believe compassion is the solution to all problems.
o   I Believe time brings about opportunity and thought.
o   I Believe I have been put on this earth and in this position for a purpose.
o   I Believe I am capable of anything as long as I have the desire to do it.
o   I Believe the choices I make are my responsibility alone.
o   I Believe I am who I am because of all the people in my life.

What do you Believe?

The saying "gratitude turns what you have into enough" is so true.

I have found the trick to practicing gratitude is to look at the most simple and mundane aspects of my life. Even in the trials of everyday life I find really good things everywhere I look. Noting each and every blessing in the things I do helps me to heal. I used to dread meal planning, grocery shopping and cooking only to have to clean up the mess after our meal. This all used to be quite overwhelming. Over time, I began to change my mindset and actually have grown to enjoy cooking. I get to help nourish my husband and my kids! This simple shift changed everything because I get to feed the ones I love. I enjoy trying new recipes and have become more adventurous. Sometimes a change of perspective is all it takes to allow gratitude to run free in any area of our lives. I figured out that once this happens everything begins looking like a great big THANK YOU. With gratitude comes an abundance of peace and healing.

My strength, compassion and belief brought me to this deep appreciation of Lyme Disease. God has blessed me in so many ways on this personal journey of healing. The lemons I already had and the lemons placed before me at the perfect moment in time are my miracles. I see them all through my Lyme-colored glasses. They refresh me like a tall glass of lemonade on a hot, summer day. It is the irony of all ironies to experience tragedy, in my case illness, and come out of it feeling more grateful and blessed than ever!

J.R.R. Tolkien:

"Faithless is he who says 'farewell' when the road darkens."

TAMARA

FINK

Tamara Fink grew up in a minister's home and defied all the stereotypes of Pastor's Kids by loving Jesus all the way through her teen years. Her love for God has grown as she has weathered storms with Him by her side. These storms and growing up in a minister's home have inspired her to share her story of hope and transparency. As her name means, Palm Tree, she longs to come alongside women and show them the gift of bending and not breaking and rising up to be stronger than ever because of the blessing of the storm.

—— Chapter 16 ——

GOOD EVENING, GOD, IT'S ME!

Tamara Fink

"Be completely humble and gentle; be patient, bearing with one another in love."

෴*Ephesians 4:2-3 (NIV)*

I don't ever remember a time not loving God.

He has always been so very real to me. I can remember as far back as snuggling into my Holly Hobbie sheets, with my mountain of stuffed animals surrounding me and my diary propped up on my knees, that I loved God. Ever since I was little, I would write. I had a diary with a little lock. Of course, like everybody else with those little diaries, I lost the key and it never locked again. I truly had childlike faith, I knew He was there. God was always there.

When I was a little girl, I hated going into our basement. It was inevitable most nights that my mom would need something from the pantry that was located under the basement stairs and send me down there to fetch it for her for dinner preparations. I had created this monster in my mind that only ate little girls with brown hair and brown eyes, ME! One such evening I ventured into the basement to get the spaghetti sauce and was running up those old linoleum clad steps when my dad sensed and heard my terror. He was waiting for me at the top of the stairs and simply reminded me that, "God is always with you. Stop running, turn around and look that monster right in the face. God won't let him get you." From then on I practiced walking those steps and staring down that monster until it was no longer necessary. I learned in those moments that fear can grip me but God never leaves me. I would walk hand in hand with him everywhere I went every day.

So, as I talked to God at night, I knew He was right there with me. I was always anxious to talk to God at the end of each of my days. He and I were the best of friends. I just knew He waited to hear from me all day and He couldn't resist listening to all of the sordid details of my day. My journal entries always started with, "Good night God, It's me!" It was an innocent closing of my day.

I would jabber on and on about boy troubles or friendship squabbles or my absolute disgust that my parents actually felt it was necessary to put a time limit on my phone time, but I also shared the deepest desires of my heart. I really cherished that time together with Him. Just Him and I. I would talk and He would listen and then He would talk and I would listen. Not talk like in audible words, but whispers directly into my heart. Words perfectly strung together in my mind that reminded me of who I was and Whose I was. That's why today; laying on the dunes, squishing the sand in my toes, listening to the waves lap on the shore, feeling the sun on my face and wind in my hair, I know His voice. It is such a familiar voice to me.

So sweet.

So gentle.

So strong.

I heard Him loud and clear with His still small voice. He was reminding me again "You are precious to me. You are beautiful. You are priceless. You are chosen. EVERY drop of my blood was poured out just for you. I would do it again and again and again."

I knew His words to be true. *How could I be this calm? How could this unshakable peace be holding me so tightly when the battle was waging all around me?*

Not five days before this I was standing in the kitchen of the log cabin finally feeling like the past two months of disjointed family living had come to an end. Our college girl was with us. My husband, John, who had been gone almost completely the last two months either flying or frantically trying to finish our cabin renovation project, was with us, and tonight would be our first night in our cabin...all five of us together at last! We had worked all day the day before cleaning and readying the cabin and moving the furniture back in. We were all anticipating tomorrow. Tomorrow was Father's Day and the big cabin reveal party with our families.

To say excitement was high was an understatement. It would better be described as a festive night. We had country music blaring through the speakers, the lake's beautiful turquoise color was shimmering like a mirror with the beginning yellows and oranges of sunset and not a ripple on it. I had just finished making the most beautiful green, crisp salad and placed it on the counter with the rest of our celebration dinner. The corn on the cob was dripping with butter, the potatoes were piping hot, and the table was set. I dreamily gazed out at the lake as I waited for John to bring the chicken in off the grill. Morgan had been pacing back and forth nervously across the deck, with what I assumed was anxious anticipation for the summer meal being prepared. Suddenly I realized, she wasn't waiting for dinner, she was sobbing inconsolably. I stood and watched for a moment as she and John seemed to be talking. I couldn't quite make out what was happening, but I could tell it wasn't going well.

Morgan is my stoic girl with controlled emotions. *What could possibly have caused her to be so upset?* I watched for a minute and nothing seemed to make sense.

I kept watching

and she kept crying

and he kept standing there limply.

My heart began to ache and race at the same time my mind began to whirl with questions. *What was happening?* I watched for a moment longer but couldn't watch anymore. I moved away from my dreamy view in the kitchen and went out onto the deck. *What could possibly have happened to my precious girl?* As I walked up to the two of them, John walked away. He walked away without even a mere glance in my direction. *What? What was going on? What had he done? Was someone hurt? Had someone died? Why couldn't my mind figure out what was going on?*

As much as I prodded and questioned Morgan she wouldn't respond. She kept sobbing and saying, "No, I can't. I can't." Finally she uttered, "I told dad."

"I told dad? I told dad what?" my mind raced. "Am I supposed to go ask dad?" I questioned.

Her body collapsed in anguished relief as she muttered, "Yes..." and sobbed some more.

I turned so quickly and abruptly I almost lost my balance. My focus was on John numbly leaning up against the counter on the other side of those screen doors. All I could think was *He is going to talk and he better not have hurt my little girl!*

I grabbed the handle on the screen door and had to control my pull as to not rip it off its runner. I stared at him waiting for him to talk. It seemed as though we were in some sort of a standoff, staring at each other, with only the nauseating meal I had prepared separating us. Staring at him, mind reeling and eyes glaring he stared back at me, empty, numb, pale and speechless. Was he seriously not going to talk? I was indignant. I was exasperated. I wanted answers.

My only thought blurted out of my mouth. "Are we getting divorced?"

Every imaginable thought was flashing through my head as he stammered, "NO!"

No.

He had answered that question far too quickly and I had asked a question of him that he was not qualified to answer. I would be the only one able to answer that question. As the events unfolded, my worst nightmare was happening again. We had already walked this path. We had already recovered from this trauma. *How could this be happening again? How God? Why God?*

In the next moments he began to ashamedly admit his unfaithfulness again. This time, it was worse though. This time I couldn't shield my girls. Morgan had found a text message on his phone. We had all been singing along to the country music blaring from his Spotify® account when she went to change the song...an accidental discovery. She had been pacing back and forth across the deck not because of anticipation for the summer meal, but because she was left to figure out what to do with the information she had just discovered. She was brave and confronted him and he walked away.

AGAIN!

NO!

I had said I would NEVER do this again. *How could this be happening to me again?* As my mind whirled and my fury raged all I could think about was my girls. *Where were my girls?* I had to get to them. Poor Morgan. *What had she seen? How could she be so incredibly brave?* As the night dragged on, and our dinner sat cold and untouched, we made calls to family asking for prayer and letting them know the celebration was off.

In all of our married lives, even after the first affair, I never asked John to leave. This would be the first night that he was made aware that he was unwelcome in our home or near any of us. It was also the first night I moved into my parent's basement and I was praying it wouldn't be permanent. They assured me we could stay as long as we needed and they would take care of us and I was a good mom and on and on, but honestly none of it was sticking. He had broken me...again.

The next day was Father's Day. It was not a day any of us wanted to acknowledge or celebrate. The day seemed to drag by. We each took turns being strong which then was exchanged for times of deep sadness, rejection, bewilderment, disbelief, tears, and more tears. There was no way out of this. I began planning in my head the sale of our home. *Where would I live? Where would I work? How could I afford to raise our daughters?* As the thoughts of doubt and fear were crashing in on me, Jana, my sister-in-law, reminded me "Today you breathe. All you need to worry about today is breathing. The rest will come."

So that's what I did.

I began to breathe.

Sleep wouldn't come.

Food wouldn't stay in.

But breathing…I could breathe.

> *Today you breathe. All you have to worry about today is breathing. The rest will come.*

As my breathing began to become natural again, the girls and I decided to move into our cabin. We had sacrificed so much already, we decided we didn't need to sacrifice that, as well. That first night in our cabin I slept so well. I felt safe and at home. I heard that familiar voice speak to me.

So sweet.

So gentle.

So strong.

I heard Him loud and clear in His still small voice. I was going to be ok. I had trusted Him all those years ago with my heart and my future. He wasn't about to let me down now.

I remember the day well. It was the fall semester of my Senior year in college. Fall truly is one of the best times in Minneapolis in my opinion. I loved the city. The sights, the sounds, the smells, my college with the ivy on the walls …I loved it all. The lights and the people-watching and the drone of the traffic, it was all very soothing to this small town girl. I felt alive and full of adventure when I was there.

Then, there was my roommate, Lisa. She was the first friend I'd ever had that loved God with her whole being. She didn't have a relationship with Him for show, but it was a true sense of longing to know Him more. She was diligent in spending time with Him and making that relationship a priority. She was externally beautiful. She literally looked like a blonde version of the Little Mermaid. She sang, and played the piano, and was super smart. She was creative and spontaneous, and fun, and genuine. She lived life to the fullest and knew how to make you feel special. Lisa had a contagious laugh and a huge toothy smile that lit up the room. We shared clothes, so much so that we bought outfits together and couldn't figure out who should take the tops or bottoms because we couldn't remember what belonged to whom by the end of the year. Lisa was the first person and the only person for a very long time that I would have given my life for. That's how deep and strong our friendship was. It was while in college, though, that I would meet the second.

I remember Lisa and I being squished in her Papasan chair for all the big talks. The window was propped open, letting the crisp night air in, along with all of sounds and smells of the city. For some reason, that Papasan chair tucked back in the corner of our wood paneled room with the rummage sale floral curtains just felt like home. It seemed to call us there to discuss the deep things of our heart. We chattered on and on about life, God and our boyfriends.

Would they propose this year? Where would we live? Would we have houses that connected our closets with a secret underground tunnel so we could share clothes forever?

As much as my heart longed to be loved and married, I had had multiple heartaches before meeting John. I was leery of giving my heart away again. We had been dating for about a year and I knew it was getting serious. I would need to decide how much longer I was going to let this relationship go on before I called it quits. The summer I met John, I was completely heartbroken and had declared to my dad I would be "the first Pentecostal nun and I was done with guys! It was gonna be me and Jesus FOREVER!" (I'm sure that wasn't a horrible thought for my dad.)

I started my summer job as a lifeguard shortly after my declaration and I met John on the very first day of orientation. He was funny and drove a motorcycle. I, however, had ridden a ten-speed bike to work that day and, as orientation dragged on, I sat on the picnic table watching the storm clouds roll in. John saw his opportunity and offered to drive me home on his buddy's crotch rocket and I couldn't resist. We became fast friends and spent every day but one together that summer. He loved motorcycles and skiing and hanging out with my family at the camp my dad directed. He even took me flying in his two-passenger plane. I thoroughly enjoyed him and was even falling for him. That was the problem. I had fallen madly in love with Jesus and didn't want anyone to distract me from that relationship. So here I sat, a year later, squished in a Papasan chair and knowing I needed to hear that familiar voice once again.

I waited for Lisa to fall asleep.

When I could hear her steady breaths I got up and snuck down the hall to the prayer room. I locked the door and grabbed my journal. It no longer had a lock, but still carried my conversations with God.

I began to scribble frantically.

"Good Night Lord, it's me! You know I love you and trust you so I'm asking you to show me what to do. I can't keep doing this with John if it's not your will. Please give me a sign. I read about Gideon in Judges and I don't know how to do this fleece thing, but it says in your word that you never change, so God, can you tell me what to do? I will do whatever you say. I trust you with my heart and I trust you with my future."

I sat....

and I waited....

and I listened....

The minutes seemed to drag on for what felt like hours, but I was patient. I knew He heard me and I was sure He was going to answer. So I waited for that familiar voice

So sweet.

So gentle.

So strong.

I heard Him loud and clear with His still small voice. "Pray that you get a letter from John's dad in three days."

What? That was the craziest thing I had ever heard. I wasn't even sure if John's dad liked me. He'd never written me a letter before. His mom had sent care packages and letters. *Could I pray for that?* I'd better pray for that! I had asked God and I had heard His answer.

What happens if you change your fleece? Can you do that? Does that nullify the fleece? Does that mean if I don't get the letter God answered the fleece or nullified the fleece?

Oh man...now I was in trouble. I had prayed the fleece and wished I hadn't because now it was too late and the countdown was on. Three days. I had three days to wait and John's dad had three days to move! The days seemed to race by and my mailbox remained empty from letters from John's dad. The third day was here. I put off going to my mailbox for as long as I could. I just wasn't ready to say goodbye. *How was I going to explain to John that we had to break up? Did I explain it or just do it?*

I slowly made the trek into the mailroom. It seemed everyone else was excitedly laughing and talking and mingling with friends, eating snacks, and sitting in booths. I felt like time was standing still. I slowly inserted the key into the tiny metal box...reminiscent of my first diary's lock. It was the third day. I turned the key and slowly, carefully opened the door. *What had I prayed? I wasn't Gideon! Did I even really know the voice of God or was that a made up voice from my childhood?* No, I knew that voice, but this voice whispering doubt, I knew that voice, too. I determined I wouldn't listen anymore and forcefully dug my hand into the mailbox. There was something in there! It was a card. I stood and stared, too shocked to look and see who it was from. It was from John's dad! Now my thoughts really began to swirl. *What did this card mean? Was I going to marry this guy?* I had never thought of that scenario. *I had trusted God with my heart and my future but was this who I had been praying for?* I ripped the card open; it was a generic card from their store with just a couple of sentences scribbled on the bottom.

Good evening Tammy,

The Lord awoke me tonight and I was praying for you.
I felt prompted to let you know. Please be careful riding your bike to work.

I love you,
John R

He had put the time and date on the top of the card and it was the same time and date that I had written in my journal. It was at the exact same time…God was whispering to me and stirring John R. from his sleep. He surely was faithful to me and I would trust Him with my heart and my future.

So, here I stand…seven days out from the horrible news and yet that familiar voice is whispering to me again.

So sweet.

So gentle.

So strong.

I hear Him loud and clear with His still small voice. "Don't rush. Take it all in. It will be too much if you rush."

So I wait.

I pause.

I take it all in.

I'm about to crest the hill to see Lake Michigan and experience the sand dunes, but I must stop. What is He saying to me?

"Can you hear it?"

Yes, I hear it. I hear the water lapping on the shore. I hear the children giggling as they run along the sand.

"What do you see?"

I see the light reflecting off the lake back up into the sky. It's a shimmering that shows that water is near.

"What do you feel?"

I feel the breeze blowing through my hair. I toss my head back and I feel the summer sun radiating on my face. I feel fully alive, fully free, and fully loved. I'm going to be ok. I slowly take another step; I can see Lake Michigan, but only a small portion. I want to see more, it wasn't enough, but I won't rush. I will take it all in. I will feel every moment. I begin to experience the vastness of Lake Michigan and the dunes. I no longer can contain my emotion. My eyes begin to weep and my body becomes weak. I walk to a solitude place and allow my body to rest in the warm sand. I let the tears fall down my cheeks. They aren't tears of sadness or rejection or betrayal. They are tears of joy, of love overflowing. I feel His soft kisses in the sweetness of the sun's rays. I could feel His passion for me in the crashing of the waves. As I sit on the dunes, I pull out my journal and prop it up my knees.

"Good night God, It's me!" I immediately hear that familiar voice.

So sweet.

So gentle.

So strong.

I hear Him loud and clear with His still small voice. He says, "I know. This time I get to talk first and you get to listen and then you talk and I'll listen."

I giggle to myself and say "Cool!"

He says, "Do you see those waves? Those waves are like my love for you. I will never stop pursuing you. Just like you can't see the ends of Lake Michigan or contain Lake Michigan or fathom the vastness of Lake Michigan, so is my love for you.

I will never stop pursuing you.

It is relentless. You are precious to me. You are beautiful. You are priceless. You are chosen. EVERY drop of my blood was poured out just for you. I would do it again and again and again. You trusted me with your heart and you trusted me with your future. I didn't pick John for you, I picked you for John. Watch as I bring complete healing and wholeness to John. It is my job and my promise to you. You are going to get to meet your husband for the first time. It is going to be a celebration."

I couldn't sit anymore. I couldn't write anymore. I had no words to say back to God. I closed my eyes and let my body sink back into the warm sand. I felt safe and secure. As the sand wiggled into every nook and cranny of my being I couldn't help but laugh.

He whispered again to me, "These grains of sand are my promises to you. I am faithful."

I kept my eyes closed and let the tears stream down my face, my hair blew in the wind and felt the sun upon my face.

I muttered back, "Ok, I'll take every one of those promises. Let's see what you got, Big Guy, when it comes to this new husband of mine."

I was confident in one thing; God had never let me down. He chose *me* for *John* and I am faithful.

This was not suppose to be the chapter I wrote for this book, but by God's incredible grace, *He allowed His Holy Spirit to blow through our marriage and remove the faulty foundation.* God is such a gracious and good God, He protected me from writing the wrong chapter. I've begun to meet my new husband and God is doing a new thing in him. The phenomenal thing about my amazing God...He's omnipresent. While He is doing a new thing in John, He is so very real to me and my girls. We know His voice. It's a familiar voice to all of us.

So sweet.

So gentle.

So strong.

We hear Him loud and clear with His still small voice. I watch them each start or end their day with something I think looks a little like, "Good Evening God, it's me!"

Sarah Dessen:

"I am coming to terms with the fact that loving someone requires a leap of faith, and that a soft landing is never guaranteed."

MARY

MARKHAM

Mary Markham is a Mentor, published poetry author, and the owner of Inspirational Visions, LLC., a Christian organization. She has a passion for writing, helping others, and sharing her simple, powerful messages. When she is not writing, she enjoys gardening, cooking, canning salsa and traveling. Mary resides with her husband Craig, in Eagle, Wisconsin. She has a daughter and son who are both married, two stepsons and Yellow Lab named "Tucker." You can contact Mary Markham at Mary@inspirationalvisionsllc.com or at: www.inspirationalvisionsllc.com.

———— Chapter 17————

INSPIRED BY AN ANGEL

Mary Markham

"The angel of the Lord encamps around those who fear Him, and delivers them."

Psalm 34:7 (ESV)

Ever wonder why a person walks into your life? Or how being in the right place at the right time changes everything?

It was a beautiful day. You could feel the warmth in the air. Bellbottom jeans out...plaid shorts, t-shirt and sandals in. *Life is good!* I thought.

But that late spring day, for this skinny, little, hazel eyed fourteen-year-old turned darker than my brunette head of hair. My smile and excitement for school to be over was gone. Where could

I go and hide from the world? Where could I hide from this deep pain that came in like an unexpected threatening storm?

Have you ever felt this alone?

Scared?

Broken?

This broken teenage girl had nowhere to go. My parents were divorced, and my father was in and out of my life. My mother did her best to raise four teenagers on her own. I heard the words "tough love" but I didn't understand what that meant. I trusted him to protect me not steal my innocence. Behind the two-story brick apartment building was a hill, trees of all sizes and at the top, a Bible Institute. Running to the largest tree I could find, I hid in my drowning tears. *I just want to die!* I thought. I felt alone with no one to turn to. Startled, I heard the words, "Are you okay?" I could barely speak and wondered where this voice was coming from. I thought I was alone. Looking up I saw an angel, with kind and loving eyes. *Instantly I became calm, as if God's loving arms wrapped around me, holding me tight and reassuring me I was safe.*

"Do you believe in God," she asked.

I replied an unshakable, "YES!"

Growing up, I believed my faith was "good enough" because I went to church with family and prayed before meals and bedtime. But this felt different. Was she real or was I imagining things because of my uncontrollable tears?

This angel was real. We sat together under the tree, and I listened as she shared her faith. I was inspired. She asked me to walk with her to the Bible Institute. Security and love overcame any doubt or fear of being with this unknown inspiration. I proceeded alongside her as we walked toward the building. "No one is allowed in the dorm rooms, but we won't be long. I have something I want to give you," she said. The hallways were darker than I imagined and although I should have been more fearful, I felt calm. *Was this real or was I dreaming?* As we approached her dorm room, she opened the door, took a few steps in, and reached over, without hesitation and handed me, her obviously cherished Bible. The inside cover read, "IN THE LIGHT THAT JESUS SAVED ME." At the top of the inside page, she wrote both our names, her phone number, and the date we met. Towards the bottom, she wrote "READ: John 3 and Romans 10:9-10" and gently handed the Bible back to me, gave me a hug, and said, "Call me anytime and Trust God. He will take care of everything."

My new inspired journey began: "If you declare with your mouth, 'Jesus is Lord,' and believe in your heart that God raised him from the dead, you will be saved." For it is with your heart that you believe and are justified, and it is with your mouth that you profess your faith and are saved." (Romans 10:9-10)

After school, I ran and sat under the protective tree, in fear of being alone in the apartment. She was there first, sitting with her boyfriend, reading his Bible. I felt it was God's way of showing me I was saved and no longer needed to hide from the world.

Ellen Bennett, my inspired angel from God, never knew the day we met was the day I was sexually abused.

I kept the secret and trusted God to protect me. I felt safer when I heard my mom say, "It's called tough love" as she kicked my oldest brother out of the apartment because of his bad choices.

I witnessed my selfless mother's faith through her words and actions. I couldn't wait to grow up and be just like her, yet I was scared my deep secret would keep me from a boyfriend, ever getting married, or having children. The few boys I dated broke up with me, without giving a reason. Feeling ugly, unloved and never good enough, I cried myself to sleep many nights, although always hearing my mom say, "You're beautiful, holy and loved."

The cycle finally broke when this skinny, little, hazel eyed brunette, fell in love and got married at twenty-one years old. Still running from my fears, I held tight to "doing" instead of "being" and losing myself and what I wanted in life.

Besides marriage, I wanted children. Hoping and praying one day God would bless me with a child. By twenty-five, I suffered two miscarriages, and watched sisters-in-law carry their babies to full term. I felt unlucky. God's sense of humor answered my plea with a "three times a charm" pregnancy. Life felt perfect as I carried this blessing from God.

Shocked by the doctor's voice on the phone, he said, "You need to see a specialist. Your baby may be deformed, have health issues, and you'll need to make a decision." *What does that mean? My inspired Angel Ellen, told me to trust God, over ten years ago...so why stop now?*

The decision was easy, I replied, "I am keeping my baby and trusting God."

"I still recommend you see the specialist," my doctor insisted.

Unfortunately, the specialist appointment was on the same brisk fall day I moved into a new home. My mom insisted on taking me. I was nervous. My hands were sweaty, and I was still adamant about my decision. *So why am I here?* We walked into a small office with a round table surrounded by hanging certificates and accolades. "Before I do any testing, I need to ask some personal family history questions. Let's begin with your mom. How many pregnancies have you had?" the doctor asked. There was a long pause and the deafening silence scared me. I knew about several miscarriages but what secret was she keeping? I looked across the table; tears streamed down her cheeks. Looking quite confused, the doctor said, "I'll leave you two alone," as he walked out. She cried harder and said, "I thought this secret would be mine until the day I died."

"Mom, what secret?"

She said, "I had a baby at sixteen years old, who died ten days after he was born of a hole in his heart. You can't tell anyone!" She wouldn't share details so I wondered if she was raped. After telling the doctor, it was up to her to share her secret.

Trusting God, my beautiful baby girl and healthy blessing, Michelle, was born on Easter Sunday.

Another sunny spring day became darker as the storm arrived at my house. Startled by a knock, my heart began beating like a drum line when I opened the door and saw this large man looking at me, the nightmare I thought was gone eleven years ago. "I hear you had a little girl," he said. My past instantly spun out of control in my head. I kept my promise all these years, and he was not going to hurt my precious baby girl. Remembering Ellen's words, "Trust God!" I took a deep breath, prayed, my hands stopped shaking, and the sick and scared feeling dissipated.

I heard every second ticking by on the clock that hung on the kitchen wall, "Tick, tick, tick..." I watched the big hand move from one minute to the next. *Okay God, I'm waiting, now what do I do?* I wondered. The sounds became deafening in my head. Actual minutes, felt like hours. His sleep apnea caused him to dose off while waiting. His body jerked, waking him as I calmly convinced him to leave. "She could sleep all day," I said. I immediately locked the door and prayed he would never return. No more dark secrets. I then called my mom and told her everything. Her expressionless voice led me to believe something about my dark secret held an even darker one others were keeping. She confronted him, only to hear, "Mary needs to get over it. It was a long time ago, and I was on drugs." As though that was his excuse for his disgusting behavior. Unfortunately, this dark secret was never to be talked about again.

Two more years passed having two more miscarriages. Although it was painful losing these babies, my faith grew, watching God work miracles in my life. My doctor, having thirteen children of his own, said, "God only gives you what you can handle and boy He must think you can handle a lot! There is a reason for everything. Trust in Him." (I heard Ellen's voice inside my head.) God's sense of humor came when my two-year-old daughter handed me baby blue golf tees. Finally, pregnant again and with only one month to go, she put her hand on my belly and said, "Mommy, baby today!"

Trusting God when the doctor asked, "Do you believe in fate?"

Do you believe in fate?

"Yes! Why?" I asked.

He insisted something was wrong with my baby. The thought of losing another child was too difficult. Repeatedly hearing the still small voice, "TRUST ME!" I trusted and was blessed with a premature little boy, who was taken away from me as quickly as he entered this world. "I'm sorry, your son is very sick and we don't think he will make it through the night," said the doctor. The pastor from our new church was called, and without hesitation he arrived. He held my hand, and we prayed throughout the night. God had a plan and purpose for this little boy, as he is now twenty-four years old, and serving as Staff Sergeant in the United States Air Force.

My dark secret continued to haunt me, causing me to become a protective parent, trusting God to teach me to pray, parent, and protect them for His purpose.

God used people in my life to help me and I saw how I could help others. "Truly I tell you, whatever you did for one of the least of these brothers and sisters of mine, you did for me." (Matthew 25:40)

My children ran into the house, "Mommy there are kids yelling in the park!"

There was a mob of about twenty-five teenagers surrounding one young girl in the park across the street. She clearly cried out, "STOP! LEAVE ME ALONE!" Without hesitation, I walked in the middle of them, and broke up the near fight. While shouted and cursed at, ignoring them, I walked up to the little girl, our eyes connected, and tears fell down her face. A flashback, looking into Ellen's eyes, is that what I looked like? Scared, yet relieved? I was grateful God put me in her life to save her from that mob.

Now, I needed an angel in my life. I was in the middle of a divorce, a stay-at-home mom, and I was alone and afraid. The phone rang and I heard the words, "You got the job!" I was numb, and not as excited as I should have been.

I politely said, "Thank you, when do I start?" I needed to trust God. Kneeling next to my bed, tears flowing, I pleaded and prayed for help. The telephone rang again, and my new neighbor said, "The Holy Spirit guided me to call you, Are you okay?" I sobbed. She was my angel. God answered my plea and showed me, once again, TRUST in HIM! My angel watched the children and refused to take any money. I knew they were safe and in God's hands.

Although God sent angels to help, I still worried. My stresses caused severe migraines, which led doctors to discover a hole in my heart. I couldn't help but wonder why my mother lost a child after ten days from a hole in his heart and here I am, still living. God has a plan and a purpose.

Living away from family and going through a divorce made me miss them even more. I needed to see my mom, who was my best friend.

I needed to see my mom, who was my best friend.

A coworker, originally from Wisconsin, told me about an airline deal. *Perfect, I'll get away from this pain and see my mom.* God was planting seeds for the next chapter of my life. Waiting for my flight to Wisconsin, I felt angry, hurt, sad, and disappointed. I thought, it's best not to talk to anyone, especially men right now. Before boarding the plane, my friend Cathy called to wish me well and to pray. After praying, she said, "Mary, God will bless you with a loving man in your life, in His time not yours." I sat next to the window and clutched my book, "A Purpose Driven Life." A tall, clean cut, dark brown receded hairline man approached my row. I thought to myself, *No way! I am not going to talk to him.* I immediately turned my head and didn't say a word. I closed my eyes and leaned on the window. I heard the pilot's voice over the loud speaker, "We have reached 30,000 feet." The man I ignored for the first hour and a half asked me what I was reading while he handed me a trail mix bar, which was given out earlier, while I was sleeping...or ignoring him. His gorgeous hazel blue eyes, and cutest chin dimple warmed my heart. He shared his story... divorced with two boys. I shared mine...going through a divorce, have a daughter and a son. We shared our faith and longed for the same things. I thought, *Really God? What is happening to me? I'm supposed to hate men right now.* He was not only good-looking, had a great smile, but was a Christian too! Many emotions spun in my head. He glanced over, with a smirk, and asked, "Would you ever move back to Wisconsin?"

My quick immediate response, was an adamant, "No! Never! I live in Colorado!"

I thought to myself, *'just because you're good looking, doesn't mean I'm going to move back to Wisconsin.'*

Was I really ignoring that still small voice, "Trust Me!" How was I trusting God when all I was thinking about were reasons I wouldn't move back to Wisconsin?

At the time, I worked at a middle school and there was some cattiness going on at the office that I didn't want to take part in. I would go back to my apartment, every day, at lunch, and get on my knees to pray. I would say, "God, if this is something you want me to do, I need answers...I need a real sign."

The conversations with the kids began to come around. Because they had moved around so much, they were adaptable. They weren't afraid of making new friends in a new place. Still, I couldn't take them away from my ex-husband. Wisconsin would never be able to happen.

"You have more family here than Colorado," Craig reminded me.

This ended up being the clincher for my ex-husband. He realized that the children would get to know all of their grandparents in Wisconsin...his parents, too. He granted me the right to move the kids out of state.

God had taken down all the barriers. He grew discontentment in me for my work environment, He reminded me of my adaptable children, and he opened the path for them to move across the country.

As a family, we prayed about moving and we kept it to ourselves until we knew that it was going to happen.

After a year of endless telephone conversations, back and forth trips, planning and trusting God, He led us, the Penske Truck and loaded car, safely to Wisconsin. When moving day came, and we drove from Colorado to Wisconsin, Craig had to listen to an audio book for work…"Good to Great". Little did he know how fitting that was! God blended our two families and four children better than many blood related siblings bonded. Repeatedly hearing, "Trust God" I questioned if there was a bigger reason why everything fell into place….

Finally, more one-on-one time with my mother. It was a sunny crisp September day, she insisted on picking me up for lunch. Looking at her as I climbed into the car, I blurted, "WOW mom, you look absolutely beautiful! What did you do different? You look like an angel!" She was glowing; beautiful as usual but that day seemed different. We laughed, cried, and reminisced about life. Gently reaching over, she grabbed my hands, looked straight into my eyes, and said things about my life, future, and people leaving me and although I would be alone, not to be scared. She said, "God gave me strength and now I am giving you all my strength."

"Mom, you're scaring me!" She took both hands placed them on my face, and said, "I love you and give you all my strength!" Then she kissed me.

The following week, she wasn't feeling well. Our year of new memories and unforgettable lunches, turned into a nightmare. Whooping and hollering for our football team to score; whistles and cheers were no longer heard after answering my telephone. The words haunted me, "Mom has pancreatic cancer." Tears flowing, I felt sick and motionless.

I can't lose my mom. NO! Not now! Not EVER!

I just moved back, and we're closer than ever! What about the kids? Their grandmother!

Oh…my head spun. *Was THIS the reason God made everything happen and moved me back to Wisconsin? Is that why my coworker told me about the flight? Is that why Craig, who is now my husband, was on that plane sitting next to me?* Our future trips and dreams were gone, forever. I felt sad, angry, devastated and alone. Wait! I thought, *Alone, is that why she told me I would be alone?* She warned me. Everything said at lunch was coming true. **God prepared her to prepare me.** Four months later, my mom passed away.

My best friend, my mother, my children's grandmother was gone forever. The children having divorced parents, living in a new state and now losing their grandmother, I worried about them. An image of Ellen handing me her cherished Bible, flashed through my head. Was I trusting and listening to the still small voice, "Let Go. Let God!"

I needed to let go and let God by living and sharing my faith, just like I witnessed Ellen doing. While witnessing my stepdad still very distraught, losing his wife of twenty-seven years, I continued to encourage him as he witnessed the change in my life and wanted to experience the same.

Then, I received a letter that changed our relationship forever. Was he lonely or just keeping a dark secret? I held the letter, and stood shocked and motionless; my chest felt tight while my heart pounded heavily. I felt anger inside and out. The open windows on that hot summer night, kept me from screaming at the top of my lungs. *What was he thinking? He must be confused and distraught over mom's death,* so I thought. How could this man, who was like a father to me, who I trusted, write such graphic and disgusting letters and emails expressing his love for me? This was a living nightmare. The kind you wake up screaming, "NO!" "STOP!" and no one hears you. *I trusted God,* and He gave me strength to end all ties with my stepdad.

It was Easter; a time of new beginnings and fond memories with my mom…Easter baskets and egg hunts. Startled by my phone ringing as I reminisced, I heard, "Our stepdad is in the hospital and dying of pancreatic cancer and is holding onto something." Standing shocked, speechless, my hands were trembling. I knew what that something was. I can't believe it was three years. Trust Me, I heard repeatedly inside my head. Okay God, I get it! I know what I need to do! My son insisted on going with me to the hospital, as though he needed to protect me from any more pain. As we walked into the room, I was overcome with a sense of peace and strength. Our eyes met; he looked ashamed as his eyes filled with tears. Hi Grandpa," Nik said as he pulled up a chair next to the bed. It was as though my son already forgave his grandpa without saying it.

"May I sit here?" I asked as I sat on the bed.

His clearly spoken words, made it hard to believe he was dying anytime soon.

Grabbing his hand, I said, "I forgive you! Please let go and let God take you!" We held hands and together recited the "Our Father" prayer. We hugged, said our goodbyes and lastly, I said, "I love you. I forgive you. It's time to let go." He passed away, on Easter Sunday.

After the loss of my mother and stepfather, I felt God's presence during the early morning hours when I had trouble sleeping. Powerful healing messages filled my heart – God was talking and I was listening. I saw messages as images of simple words that spoke volumes; "Let Go Let God," "I AM," and "Broken Not Shattered." God created these images, thus creating Inspirational Visions, LLC, where each person takes away what they need to for whatever they are going through.

These powerful messages helped me let go and let God. At a family gathering, face-to-face with my past, my heart at peace and no longer feeling threatened, I walked up to my abuser, put my hand on his shoulder; I felt stares from across the room, and I whispered, "I forgive you" and gave him a hug. It was the first and only time I witnessed tears of remorse for what he had done to me at age fourteen. God taught me to trust Him in everything in life. "For everything there is a season, and a time for every matter under heaven…moreover, it is God's gift that all should eat, and drink, and take pleasure in their toil." Ecclesiastes 3:1, 3:13

At peace with one last step to let go, I drove slowly down the road and stopped where it all began. The apartment building demolished, leaving only a large slab of concrete. God blessed, strengthened and gave me hope through each miracle. How different would my life have been had I not trusted God, listened to the still small voice or been inspired by my angel, Ellen, through all my life's challenges. When and where will your angel inspire you? With God, all things are possible.

God made us all beautiful, holy and loved.

Ian Thomas:

"To be in Christ, that is redemption; but for Christ to be in you, that is sanctification!"

JULIE

NOWAK

Julie Nowak is a dedicated mother to her three adopted children, Charles (12), Isabelle (11), and Addisyn (9). She and her kids currently reside in Pewaukee, Wisconsin. If Julie is not Assisting in Surgery at the Hospital where she has been working for over twenty-six years, she can be found hanging out with her kids, attending a large variety of activities and sports they participate in. This is Julie's first publication and she is thrilled to be a part of such an inspiring and Faith-based book. You can contact Julie at julienowak@hotmail.com.

—— Chapter 18 ——

ABUNDANTLY BLESSED

Julie Nowak

"Trust in the Lord with all your heart and lean not on your own understanding."

༝ *Proverbs 3:5 (NIV)*

For as long as I can remember, I've always had an enormous love for children. I grew up the third child of four, and my parents loved us all with everything they had. Soon after we were in school my mom started a day care service in our home, and I absolutely loved helping out with the kids. I couldn't wait to get home from school so I could play with the toddlers or feed and rock the babies. I told myself from early on that I was going to have a huge family; the more kiddos the better!

As the years went by my love for children never faded, and my passion for a career was also ignited. I finished high school and headed to the University of Wisconsin Stevens Point (UWSP) to begin my studies in the field of Biology and Physiology. I had dreams of becoming a doctor one day and helping people around the world. "Dream big or go home, right?" As a three sport athlete all through high school, I naturally gravitated toward the softball field and the basketball court at UWSP. I spent my extra time in the gym and met so many talented female athletes. I lived in the dorms my first year and experienced total freedom and independence and had so much fun, I started to lose sight of my hopes and dreams. I began to spend more time hanging out with friends and less and less time studying. I found myself on academic probation and by the middle of my sophomore year I managed to flunk out. I was in shock.

How could I let that happen? I was determined to do whatever it took to get back into school so I could realize my forgotten dreams. With the support of my parents and letters from my basketball coach and a few professors, I received a second chance. This whole ordeal threatened my confidence and self–esteem, and I turned to food and friends to get me through.

As I gained weight, I began to question myself and I started to doubt if I would ever see my dreams come true.

I headed home for the summer and worked in two different factory jobs, one by day and the other at night. The people I worked with were tons of fun, and we would often go out after our shift ended. I had a blast and even met a guy who was super sweet, so sweet he said to me, "You'd be such a beautiful gal if only you would lose some weight." Although true, those words really hurt.

With the crisp autumn air setting in, I returned to school and this time moved into an apartment with a good friend from the basketball team. I have always been very accepting of everyone, no matter who they were or what they did, so—when my good friend told me she was a lesbian and wanted me to meet her girlfriend—I was very supportive. The next thing I knew I was going to all female parties. I didn't think much of it, after all I had a lot of friends who were gay and I was raised to "judge not, and you shall not be judged." I quickly became so accepting of my friends, I even stood up in a union ceremony. I remember as I thought to myself, what are you doing and what would mom and dad think if they knew what you were doing?"

> *Judge not and you shall not be judged.*

I left Stevens Point and moved back home and felt very defeated so when a gal from school called and asked if she could hang out with me on her way through town I was excited to have a visitor. When she told me I was amazing and had a great smile I couldn't help but feel incredibly flattered. Before long, I found myself in and out of relationships with a couple of women; my life was nothing like I had planned. My parents were so unbelievably disappointed in me and my lifestyle choices, not to mention, totally embarrassed, I'm sure. I began to live somewhat of a double life. I had gotten a new job, and no one there knew anything about my relationship. I liked it that way. As a very private person, it wasn't hard for me to keep that part of my life to myself.

Years went by and I was so caught up in my relationship, I sold my house and moved three hours away to start our new life together. It wasn't long after I moved in that I realized I had made a huge mistake. I discovered that she was already talking to other women online. I had never felt so lonely in my entire life. I began to experience real pain and was not feeling well at all. I scheduled an appointment to see my regular doctor back home, and a series of tests showed I had a very fast growing fibroid cyst on my uterus. I needed to have surgery relatively soon. As I left the hospital, I felt overwhelmed and began to pray. This was something I hadn't done in awhile. I mean, *I know our God is a loving God.* I believed with all of the hate, war, hunger and hurt in the world, how could being in a loving relationship be wrong? What did God think of me? I knew my family did not approve of my situation at all.

The next day I got home from work and got on the computer. I checked my emails and saw that I had received an email from my old boss asking me how I was doing. He let me know I could always have my job back if I wanted it. Wow, this was the push I needed to tell my partner that I felt like I needed to move back home and take my boss up on this offer to get my job back. My partner was pretty upset, but knew it was something I needed to do. She made the decision to sell her house and move with me; she would quit her job of several years to live with me and go back to school to get another degree. I was very uneasy about this situation, but I also didn't like conflict and I thought this could be a good opportunity for both of us.

My gay life was about to collide with my straight life, and I was petrified! The questions I would have to answer questions from co-workers and friends about who this woman was and what was her relationship to me? This was an area that was always a struggle for me. My partner was extremely confident in her identity as a lesbian and I was not. She couldn't understand why I was always so hesitant to talk about our relationship openly.

With this invasive surgery, not only did they remove this massive fibroid but I needed to have a total hysterectomy which left me completely devastated. My dream of having lots of kids came to a

My dream of having lots of kids came to a screeching halt.

screeching halt. How could this happen to me? Was God punishing me for my lifestyle choices? I was in so much pain physically and emotionally. I had an emptiness inside with feelings of enormous loss. I felt as if no one really cared or understood though because I wasn't married. I believed I was not worthy of true happiness. My pain was intensified when my sister announce she was pregnant. I desperately wanted to be happy for her but that happiness escaped me. Neither my partner nor I was happy in our relationship but I avoided that pain as well.

I was pretty confident that no man on earth would ever want to be with an overweight woman who wasn't able to have children, not to mention, I was living with a woman. It was time for me to accept the fact that I would never have the life I had always dreamed of. I needed to find happiness in the life that I had.

I began to pray again. I believed God was disappointed in me so I basically spent my prayer time begging Him to give me strength and guidance in my life. I couldn't believe God would take away the one thing I so desperately wanted so I began to look at other ways I could impact a child's life. I researched foreign adoptions and how I could make that a possibility. I then shared my new hopes and dreams with my partner, and she quickly shot me down. Once again I felt defeated, rejected and punished.

A dear friend of mine saw I was hurting and told me how she and her partner were going through the process of dual licensing to become foster parents with the option to adopt. I knew right away I wanted to do this. My partner and I continued to struggle with our situation but I believed she knew I was determined to make a difference in the life of a child. This was when I gave her the ultimatum. I am doing this with or without you so if you want out, this is your chance. She had every excuse in the book as to why is wasn't a good time to do this but I wasn't backing down. We started the thirty-six hours of training and all the home study preparations. Three months later we completed the requirements and got our foster care licenses. I received my dual license and could adopt as well. There are really no words to describe how happy and overjoyed I was to know that is was only a matter of time before a child would be coming into our home. However, my family was not overly excited, which caused doubts in my mind if I was doing the right thing.

I didn't have long to ponder the situation because three days after we got our license, we received "the call" about a premature baby boy. This little guy was so tiny and very sick. He needed a great deal of extra care to nurse him back to health. We went up to the hospital the next day to meet this beautiful, precious little guy who was hooked up to monitors and had oxygen tubes securely taped to his tiny little face. He was truly a gift from God! As I held him and fed him I couldn't help but wonder if this little life would forever be a part of my life. I instantly began to pray for his precious little body to have strength and for God to heal him. It was in this moment that I knew I was meant to be a mom; this amazing little boy and making sure he had everything he needed to be healthy became my only focuses.

Like most dysfunctional relationships, we coasted along. She in her new job, and I was completely focused on this baby boy. It was easy to forget that I still needed to figure out who I was and what God's plans were for me. One thing I knew for sure was that I wanted to help more children in my life. I also knew my partner did not want to have any more kids. Would this be the factor that would separate us? After much discussion she ultimately said she would let me have one more child, so I called children's social services and told them I was ready for another placement. Within two weeks I was called about a little girl who was living with her grandma and needed some help. She was a gorgeous eleven month old who stole my heart from day one. This kiddo would be eligible for adoption and it was a total no brainer that I would adopt her as well.

This was such a difficult time for me. I was so happy to have these beautiful children in my life but my relationship with my partner was getting more challenging. My job was also very stressful, and we were trialing a new cardiac product that I needed to get trained on so I could teach the rest of the team. The next day a sales rep arrived at the hospital to help me and the team with this new product. He was extremely nice and helpful. There was just something about him; he stood out from the other reps. He was very personable and a pleasure to work with. It wasn't unusual for a sales rep to have a training session at a restaurant so when I got an email from him inviting me to dinner I didn't think anything of it, at least not until I got to the restaurant and realized I was the only person he had invited. We sat and talked over dinner and he was so easy to hold a conversation with. We talked about our kids, and he shared details with me about his daughter and her special needs. He even talked about his ex-wife, and I felt this overwhelming need to share with him that I was living with another woman. This information did not seem to bother him at all; in fact he reached across the table for my hand and said he could tell my situation was painful for me to talk about. Okay, is it just me? What guy does that? I could feel my eyes welling up with tears, and I became at a loss for words at which time he began to tell me how beautiful I was and that I really didn't fit the image he had of a lesbian. I smiled and thought I truly never felt like I fit into that mold. After talking for what seemed like hours, we left the restaurant and he walked me to my car. He gently grabbed my hands, leaned in, kissed me on the forehead and asked if we could do this again sometime. I smiled, I'm pretty sure from ear to ear, and told him I was definitely not happy in my situation but I also needed to deal with it and figure things out before we could go on another date together.

As I drove home that night I couldn't help but think that God must have sent this man into my life to bring me clarity and give me the feelings of hope and freedom from a life I felt so alone in. He took all of my doubts about finding a man who would see me for who I was and still find beauty. I really felt God's presence in my life in that very moment, and I knew in an instant what I needed to do.

I immediately told my partner that we needed to talk, and she totally agreed. Later that week we went out for dinner and discussed how unhappy we both were in our situation. She made arrangements to move out of the house that I owned.

About a month after she left, I took my kids to a park where we met my sister and her children. I was feeling really good about everything. As we talked and watched the kids play, my phone rang. My sister noticed I was hearing some big news, and quickly asked me what was going on? As I hung up the phone I told her, you are not going to believe this…my daughter's birth mom had another baby. My daughter had a little sister! I couldn't help but smile, and although most of my family thought I was completely out of my mind to even think about being a single parent to a three year old, a barely two year old and a new infant I couldn't stand the thought of these two sisters growing up apart. Believe me, I prayed like crazy about this situation and somehow I just knew I could do it. I had absolutely no idea how I was going to do it but I knew I would figure it out. God would not have had this women call me if He didn't think I could handle it, right? This child has been an amazing addition to our family.

Now, I bet you are wondering what happened with the sales rep. We met a few more times over lunch and went out on an official date when my youngest was about eight months old. He was amazing and we got along so well. We had so much in common. The challenge was that he lived six and a half hours away and, soon after our date, he was transferred to another region. He no longer was a rep for the hospital where I worked. We stayed in touch for awhile, and then he disappeared, I could no longer reach him. He was not on any social media sites. He doesn't show up in any online searches. I even checked the obituaries just to make sure nothing happened to him. I began to wonder if he was just put into my life to again help me to see that the lifestyle I had lived for so long was based on convenience and insecurity. He knew I would never want to knowingly hurt someone and that I was willing to sacrifice my own happiness to avoid causing hurt at all costs.

This was by far the most difficult time in my life. Not only had I had a relationship with another woman but I also developed a love for her family. Her parents are amazing and her siblings were always so supportive and loving to me. Although I was never really married I did go through what felt like a horrible divorce. I am so grateful that God took me by the hand and walked with me as I went through this. As much as I felt like I was being punished and as much as I questioned God and His will for my life, it wasn't until I fully put my trust in Him that things started to change. I heard his voice guiding me and giving me strength and courage.

I feel like it truly took a miracle to set me free from so much pain, hurt and unhappiness. While I am still an overweight single mom, I am abundantly blessed and trusting that God's perfect plan will continue to unfold in my life…in His perfect timing.

Corrie Ten Boom:

"Never be afraid to trust an unknown future to a known God."

WENDY
LEPPERT

Wendy Leppert has a passion for helping and serving others. This led her to partner with her Mom and open a café in her hometown of Everett, Pennsylvania. She considers her faith, family and reaching out to help others to be the most important aspects of her life. In 1995, she married her best friend, Chad, and they have been blessed with a son and three daughters, ranging in age from nineteen to seven. She is anxious to pursue authoring more books in the future. You can contact her at cwleppert@comcast.net or reach out to her on Facebook® or Instagram®.

—— Chapter 19 ——

CRY OUT TO JESUS

Wendy Leppert

"Dear friend, I pray that you may enjoy good health and that all may go well with you, even as your soul is getting along well."

&3 John 2 (NIV)

*C*ancer.

Never did I think I would hear that word from a doctor, but there I sat, staring at him in disbelief. Suddenly, I became aware of the noisy paper I was sitting on and the lights in the ceiling became indistinct, as my eyes filled with tears. My life, up until hearing that word, was ordinary by the world's standards.

~~~~

My husband and I met when we were teenagers and we married when I was twenty-one and he was twenty-three. Three years later, we had our first child, our son, Cale. Twenty-two months after that, we had our daughter, Caylen. Having these two little children kept us busy and we use to joke that we were the "all-American family", with one boy and one girl. We had the children we always wanted and life was perfect. As they grew up, and weren't toddlers, anymore, I gained freedom in not having to follow them everywhere for safety. We could go on little day trips. Everything was as we pictured it, as we imagined it. Before we knew it, they were seven and five and—in our mind—we were set. We were good to go. I was perfectly satisfied with our family...until my daughter stepped on to the school bus for her first day of Kindergarten; that's when reality began to sink in that I no longer had a baby in the house.

I approached my husband with the notion that I would really like another child and his response was "Are you crazy? We have one of each and they're finally at the age where we don't have to follow them around every second of the day."

I couldn't help the distressing thinking that I needed another child. My husband finally agreed and about thirteen months after Caylen's first day of school, our daughter Cali was born. She was full-term but very undersized, weighing in at just over four pounds. I noticed right away that she wasn't crying when she was born and I didn't understand what was going on. I saw the worried looks on the faces of my mom and husband. That's when the doctors told me that the cord was wrapped around her neck three times. Finally, a small little whimper came from her and she was crying. I think we all breathed a sigh of relief as they took her out to clean her up.

Shortly after my mom and husband left, I was ready for some rest. Just then, the pediatric doctor came bursting into my room and told me that she was concerned about how little my baby was and that she appeared to have a spot on her lungs. She informed me that she was going to transport her to the Neonatal Intensive Care Unit (NICU) in a bigger, better-equipped hospital an hour away. I was frantic and my head was spinning with all the information she was telling me. She was talking as if she wasn't sure Cali was going to survive or not. I tried to call my husband and mom but I couldn't get the phone in my room to work. Finally, a nurse came and helped me dial out.

I remember putting my hand on her chest and crying, thinking that I was never going to see this baby grow up.

They had just left when my mom and husband were back once more. We went to the nursery where the transport team from the other hospital was working on transferring Cali to their incubator. I remember putting my hand on her chest and crying, thinking that I was never going to see this baby grow up. I couldn't believe this was happening. I sat in my wheelchair out in the hallway as they wheeled her away. The hardest part was that I couldn't even go with her. The doctor wouldn't allow me to be discharged until the next day.

That night was one of the worst nights of my life. I cried the entire night while my mom and husband were calling people and asking them to please pray for our baby. Finally, the next morning, I called over to the hospital, fearful of what they might tell me. They assured me that she was going to be fine, but she would spend her first week of life in NICU and we were so happy to finally bring her home. We hadn't told our older two that she was coming home, so they were surprised when they came home after school only to see her in the bassinet in our living room. My doctor later told me the fact that she survived without receiving any nourishment from me for so long, because of the cord around her neck like it was, was a miracle. It wouldn't be the last miracle in my body, though.

When Cali was two years old, I approached my husband and told him that Cali would also need a sibling close to her age to play with. Thank the good Lord that my husband has a sense of humor and is compassionate and understanding towards me. In October of 2008, I found out I was pregnant. Unfortunately, that excitement only lasted about two weeks, as I suffered a miscarriage. I was devastated. I didn't understand how I could have three perfectly healthy children and then lose one like this.

I had gone to my doctor's appointment unaccompanied and, after he confirmed my miscarriage, I remember sitting out in the parking lot, crying, talking to God, and telling Him, *"I still love You and I know Your ways are right"*.

His ways led to February of 2010, on the day before my 36th birthday, when I gave birth to yet another girl, Caydi. Weighing 8 lbs. 6 oz., we joked that she was the size of two Cali's! My pregnancy with Caydi was flawless and I was so thankful to God for blessing us with her after suffering the loss of a baby with my last pregnancy.

I decided to have my tubes tied the same day that Caydi was born. My uterus had been through enough, I thought. Besides my five pregnancies and four live births, all of my life, I suffered with extremely painful, heavy cycles. It seemed like after the birth of

Caydi, they got worse and I noticed the pain was especially uncomfortable on my right side.

My doctor had suggested an "Endometrial Ablation", which is a procedure that surgically destroys the lining of the uterus to bring relief to women having the same problems as me. I had three of these performed; none of them was successful.

After a few doctor visits, it was discovered that I had a Fibroid Tumor on the right side of my uterus and that my uterus was tilted; he believed this is what was causing me the pain. After discussing with my physician, we both agreed that a hysterectomy was the only way I would get relief from this.

I hated the thought of having my uterus removed. I remember crying to my husband, "But that's where our kids "lived" while I carried them for the nine months!" It seemed like a meaningless thought, but for some strange reason, it made me unhappy. I also had the expected thoughts that having my uterus removed would make me feel like less of a woman.

I struggled with these feelings and didn't take the decision lightly, but after much contemplation, discussion, and prayer, I decided to have it done. It was October 2012 and we decided to do it in December; I would be off work for a few weeks and I knew mobility would be difficult at first, so with my husband and kids off over Christmas vacation, it seemed like reasonable timing. They scheduled the procedure for December 18, 2012, my husband's forty first birthday.

My husband was struggling with his own thoughts...something that had nothing to do with my hysterectomy. In fact, he had mentioned the feeling before we even knew I would be having the procedure. He said that he kept getting a strange feeling like something bad was going to happen soon to either one of us or one of the kids. He had no idea why, it was just a feeling that he couldn't get rid of. We both just brushed it aside, hoping it was nothing.

I had my pre-operative appointments with the doctor and at the hospital. My doctor told me that he would be performing the surgery using an innovative procedure where it would be done laparoscopically, using "robotic assisted surgery". This helps the surgeon have a better range of motion as the robot translates the doctor's hand movements into smaller, more exact movements of tiny instruments inside the body. The incision is smaller and the recuperation time for a patient is quicker.

In the week leading up to the surgery, I noticed my stomach getting bigger. Because of the tumor, I always felt a little bloated, but this was different. My stomach felt solid and like I was pregnant. Even my family and co-workers noticed how large my stomach looked. By now, I could not wait to have this surgery completed to feel relieved of this "thing" that was now making me very uncomfortable.

The day of my surgery, my husband, mom and I arrived at the hospital, I was prepped, and then we waited. My pastor came to see me before I went down for surgery and read from the Bible. He particularly wanted to read to me one of his favorite verses for upcoming surgeries or looming situations.

"When you pass through the waters, I will be with you; and through the rivers, they shall not overflow you. When you walk through the fire, you shall not be burned, nor shall the flame scorch you."

~Isaiah 43:2 (NIV)

He then prayed and went out to the waiting room where he would stay to wait with my mom and husband while I was having the surgery. I hugged my mom and kissed my husband, while teasing him that because I wasn't allowed any jewelry and wasn't wearing my wedding ring, the doctors would be trying to get my phone number. I was wheeled me down to the holding vicinity asked a million questions (that they had just asked me upstairs), had an attractive shower cap slapped on my head, and was covered with a heated blanket.

The doctor, who was known for successfully performing the robot surgery, asked if I was ready to get this resolved. I said, "Oh my, yes! I feel pregnant!"

He looked perplexed and touched my stomach. His eyes became large and he informed me he was going to do an ultrasound before he performed the surgery, because it seemed a lot larger than my last visit. I remember thinking, 'Well, there goes the small incision surgery and I'll probably end up being cut wide open.' After having four kids the natural way, this conception wasn't appealing to me.

He returned with the ultrasound machine and started to analyze my stomach on the screen. He kept rubbing it over my entire stomach and his eyebrows were wrinkled, so I had a feeling he didn't like what he was seeing.

He turned the machine off and leaned on the rail of the bed. "I feel terrible telling you this, but I am not able to perform the surgery."

I was bewildered and didn't understand what was happening, I asked him, "What do you mean?" and he informed me that the tumor had grown significantly, so that he was unable to perform the surgery laparoscopically. He had never seen this type of tumor grow this considerably in size before and wanted to confirm it was nothing serious.

Feelings of disappointment and apprehension started to overwhelm me at that moment. I had been prepared, not only medically, but also emotionally, for this procedure and not having it done at the last minute like this was really a disappointment. I was also questioning what he meant by confirming it wasn't anything serious. I could see he was concerned.

I was wheeled back upstairs to the room so I could get dressed and leave for my doctor's office, where he would review the circumstances with me. My mom and husband then arrived back to the room and I already had the tears flowing.

They saw me crying and told me it was okay and the doctor explained to them that it had grown rapidly and he wanted to take a better look at it. They asked what had upset and I told them how worried the doctor looked and that he mentioned it could be something serious.

Then it hit me; I glanced at my husband and remembered the feelings he had been having these past months that something terrible was going to happen to one of us and suddenly, I hugged him saying, "What if this is cancer and the feeling you were having is because this is my last Christmas with you and the kids?"

He hugged me back and I could tell that he was now thinking this might explain the strange feelings he had been having.

We gathered my belongings and went to meet with the surgeon. He said, after consulting with my doctor, they both decided that neither of them felt comfortable performing the surgery because the "mass" would need to be sent to Pittsburgh for testing to see if it was cancerous. This was something they wanted to be able to do swiftly, so having the surgery performed there seemed more logical.

They knew an Oncologist in Pittsburgh that was very successful with these surgeries and he scheduled appointments once a month in our area. Coincidentally, the next day is when he was due to come in and he had agreed to squeeze me in between appointments. I say "coincidentally" because I feel this was all in God's plan and His schedule of occurrences for this situation in my life. My doctor told us it was quite serious and we suspected he was also considering cancer.

On the way home, my co-worker called to see how the surgery went, I cried, explaining to her what had happened. "Please just pray" I begged her.

The next morning, we were preparing to leave to meet the Oncologist. My mom was to meet up with us to ride along to the appointment, but she called saying that she hadn't slept the night before and she was crying, telling me that it was impossible for her to go along. My dad took the telephone and told me he was praying for me, mom would be okay, and they love me. My family is very close-knit, so when one suffers it distresses us all.

My parents married young, they were fifteen and sixteen, and—a few months later—I came along. I am so proud of them for staying married and fighting through the tough times. The early years were challenging, but when they resolved to make God the center of their marriage, that carried them through. My brother was born when I was ten years old and, because my mothering intuitions came out when he was born, I took great care of him and we still remain very close today. He is now married and has given me the privilege of being an aunt to his daughter and son.

We arrived at the doctor's office, walked into the waiting room, signed in, and sat down to wait to meet the doctor. As I sat there, I spotted people arriving with scarves on their heads and they were entering the room where chemotherapy was being given. I remember thinking that someday that might be me.

We went back to be introduced to the Oncologist and he explained what my doctor had already explained to us...that the mass was very sizable and he would have to make a large incision to remove it. He inquired as to whether I had any questions and my first was what could cause it to grow this large so quickly. He exclaimed, "Cancer!" and said that when it grows this large and this rapidly, it characteristically is because it's a cancerous mass.

I sensed my heart beating out of my chest and my head started to spin and immediately I thought of my four children.

How could this be happening?

I couldn't understand what I was hearing.

I felt as though life as I knew it was finished.

Would I live to see my kids grow up?

He wanted to schedule the surgery immediately; he called his nurse and instructed her to rotate appointments so he could perform the procedure on me right away. He began to inform me that he would have a pathology team in the operating room with him to examine the mass so he would know right away if it was cancerous.

He mentioned he would like to start the chemo treatments right away, but I couldn't understand anything he was saying because I suddenly felt like I was in a nightmare and everything was muddled. He scheduled me for 7:30 the next morning and requested that I arrive at 5:00 AM. This was a two-hour drive for us, which meant we would be leaving around 3:00 AM the next morning. Honestly, it was all fuzzy to me as I got my belongings together and left.

My dad requested I call him immediately after meeting with the doctor. Mom answered the phone wanting to know what he had said. I told her that, because of its size, he scheduled the surgery for the next day. As expected, she asked if he thought it was cancer. I pretended to shrug it off with her, telling her he didn't say for certain, but he just wanted to have it taken out immediately. The last thing I wanted was to tell her was that he had confirmed his thoughts to me that it was cancer.

That evening, I had so many things to complete. My children had Christmas parties coming up and we had to arrange for someone to make sure they got to their destinations. I had to go to the pharmacy to get some medications to immediately consume so that I was "cleaned out" for the surgery. I was miserable.

I was always the one who would encourage others. If my children were sick or distraught or someone I knew was struggling with something, I felt determined to make them feel better and smile through the difficulties.

Why was it so challenging when I was the one struggling? I knew that God was in control and that this was not a surprise to Him. I didn't like how everything in my life, at that moment, felt like it was spiraling out of control.

We sat our two older children down in the living room and explained to them what had happened and what the doctor had told me. I wanted to be honest with them and I let them know that cancer was a possibility. Their eyes grew big and teary when I mentioned the "C" word. At ages fourteen and twelve, they were old enough to know the seriousness of the situation and I could tell they were worried. On the other hand, when I talked to my two younger children, I had to hide the tears and make light of it. I simply told them that Mommy had something in her belly that needed taken out and I would have to be at the hospital for a few days.

We have a tradition at bedtime every night with our kids. We sit down together as a family and take turns praying. This night's prayer, however, was different. I looked around at my husband and kids and thought about all the nights we had gathered for prayer and I had simply taken it for granted. I took for granted the fact that we would always be together as a family, that my husband and I would grow old together and that I would see each one of my children grow up. In the past, it had just been a time to sit down together and pray. This time, I wanted to freeze time and cherish every second just looking at each one of them and soaking up the time together as family. I cried the whole way through the prayer.

> *I looked around at my husband and kids and thought about all the nights we had gathered for prayer and I had simply taken it for granted.*

My six-year-old gave me one of her stuffed animals to take to the hospital. I embraced my oldest two and squeezed extra hard. I went in to my two-year old's room and hugged her tight, trying to hide the tears. When hugging my six-year-old, I had trouble letting go of her as her little hand rubbed my neck.

The thought of missing my kids grow up was so overwhelming to me at that moment that I just wished I would wake up from this nightmare. The thought that it took something like this to truly absorb and appreciate every moment with them was nearly unbearable. I had let too much time go by, taking them, all of them and my husband, for granted. We are gifted our families and should cling closely to them. I stood in the kitchen, sobbing and hugging my husband, telling him "I can't do this" and *"Please don't make me do this."*

He assured me it was going to be fine, but I saw the tears in his eyes and knew he was worried too.

Because of the medicine I had to drink for surgery, I didn't sleep much that evening and had to wake up early so I felt like I hadn't slept at all. I remember getting ready in my bathroom with such a feeling of trepidation and wondering how I was going to make the two-hour trip since the drink had made me so nauseous.

Suddenly, every thought and feeling of wretchedness and anxiety that I had experienced became so overwhelming that I felt as if I couldn't stand anymore and I collapsed on the bathroom floor, sobbing and praying "God, I can't do this. Please be with me and help me get through this, I can't do this alone. I love You and I am so frightened. Please don't let this be cancer".

A feeling of warmth came over me, as if He was hugging me and whispering that everything was going to be okay. Just as abruptly as the tears developed, they went away. I stopped crying and I slowly stood up, feeling an enormous weight lifted off me. The nausea immediately stopped. I still can't explain how my tears dried up immediately and I felt this sudden eruption of strength.

My mom came with my husband and I to the hospital and we arrived to find a couple from our church was there. While we waited in the waiting room, they read from the Bible and prayed.

The nurse called my name and I hugged my mom, while my husband came back with me.

I was prepped...again...and we waited for the nurses to take me down for the procedure. When they arrived, I'll never forget the look in my husband's eyes as he squeezed my hand and kissed me on the forehead. He stood and watched them wheel me around the corner. They had already given me the anesthesia, so that corner was the last thing I remembered seeing.

"Mrs. Leppert, wake up". I heard the voice but couldn't figure out where I was and I remember thinking that I was sleeping so well and I really didn't want to open my eyes. "Mrs. Leppert, wake up. Your surgery is all done". I opened my eyes and everything was blurry. I saw the forms of two women tending to me and the one said, "We have good news – it wasn't cancer".

"Praise God!" I said and one of the ladies said, "You got that right!" I felt such happiness and tremendous liberation. I was drifting in and out, but I remember my mind repeating, "Thank You, Lord. Thank You so much!"

When I completed recovery, they wheeled me up to my room. In the doorway, stood my mom and husband. They were smiling and I could feel my own smile stretch from ear to ear. "Did you hear?" I asked them. They both nodded and we hugged.

The relief and happiness that we all felt was undeniable.

The doctor had told my mom and husband that he had never witnessed anything like what I had. He called it a "monster" and told them that it was five pieces lumped together and was soft and yellow, which normally indicates cancer. He was flabbergasted and didn't believe the Pathology team when they informed him that it wasn't cancer. He made them retest it.

Three days later, I surprised my kids by coming home. I hugged them so tight and was beyond excited to see them! The day after Christmas, the doctor called to tell me that the official testing on the mass was complete and it was confirmed that it wasn't cancer.

He told me it weighed over five pounds! My third child weighed less when she was born, so—in reality—I "delivered" a mass that weighed more than my child!

I will forever be grateful to the Lord. This experience, and the experience He kept away from me, would forever change my life. I was taught to never take anything or anyone in my life for granted. In an instant, everything can change.

The biggest lesson that I was taught is that we cannot handle trials in life alone. He is there for us, if we just reach out to Him, even when we are so distraught and can't put into words in a prayer how we feel, He hears us. He loves us more than we can ever understand; if we just cry out to Him, He is there to give us strength, hope, and love like no other we have ever experienced.

My mind often wanders back to the verse that my pastor read to me the morning I was initially to have my surgery – *"When you pass through the waters, I will be with you; and through the rivers, they shall not overflow you. When you walk through the fire, you shall not be burned, nor shall the flame scorch you."*

I passed through the fire and Cancer did not scorch me. I came out clinging more strongly than ever to the blessings He's given me.

Ben Carson:

"You can understand why I'm a believer. I have seen miracles."

DENISE

COOP

Denise Coop is a wife to Blake and a mom to Samantha, Sydney, Parker, and Zoe. Her family resides in Northern Kentucky. She believes in the statement "leader of one, leader of many". Denise thrives on intentionally growing herself daily; as she desires to become the leader that God designed her to be. Her passion is connecting God's Word to women's hearts through leading bible studies. She loves watching God change things. You can reach Denise at denise.coop43@gmail.com.

—— Chapter 20 ——

JESUS CHANGES THINGS

Denise Coop

"...you are worried and upset about many things, but few things are needed—or indeed only one."

❧Luke 10:41b-42a (NIV)

I

It is 8:45 p.m.

Softball practice ran long.

I smell.

Ten ladies will be here in fifteen minutes.

The kids are still up and wandering everywhere.

The family room is a mess.

The couch is old and falling apart.

My shelves are empty.

I can write my name in the coffee table dust.

No amount of rearranging pillows seems to help.

I need to hurry and vacuum the carpet.

Where *is* the vacuum?

Why do I *even* do this?

Have you ever stacked your commitments so close you don't even have time to breathe? I always get crazy before people come over. I have to remind myself of the bigger picture.

People matter more than a clean and perfectly decorated home.

Tonight is special. Church announced we would be reading *Favor with Kings* (by Caleb Anderson) this summer. I love doing life with my friends so I asked them if they wanted to read the book together. My friends are kind and encouraging and FUN. In the past, we have usually kept our circle tight and study with each other. This book will be different because my friends have invited their friends and neighbors to come over too. I don't know most of them and that makes me nervous. Once I get over myself and my messy house, my mind calms down and my heart swells with the anticipation of women connecting over Jesus.

Jesus changes things.

He changed everything for me.

February in west Michigan can be brutal and it felt like I hadn't seen the sun since October. I was really looking forward to getting out of work on time and spend some quality time with Blake, my husband of two and a half years. He had been traveling and I was working crazy hours trying to get promoted. As I rounded the corner into the office of the manufacturing facility, my thoughts were laser-focused on my future. I was hoping I would get the promotion to Lean Manufacturing Engineer. I had been graduated from college and working at Delphi for three years. Clearly, it was time for a change. Being just an Industrial Engineer was getting boring. The same departments, the boring paperwork, and the overwhelming expectations were starting to eat at my soul. I wanted out and I wanted change and I wanted it yesterday.

I sat down at my gray desk and checked my TO-DO LIST. I went to work. My list was getting too long again which meant I'd need to work late. I really wanted to spend time with Blake, but he would understand if I was late...again. My thoughts immediately went back to the promotion *I* wanted. If I worked late, people noticed *my* determination and commitment (to *my* goals). I was getting used to putting in forty-five to fifty-five hours a week. Blake could get used to it, too.

As I was working, my co-worker and friend, Janet, stopped by my desk. She asked me if I had ever heard of a conference called *Born to Win* in Dallas, Texas. I hadn't. She thought it would be good for me to go, but didn't give me very much information. To be honest, I didn't need to know anything other than it was in Dallas in March and it lasted for three days. This was perfect timing. I was already dreaming of a short break from the snow, a little sunshine, and time away from my departments. I sent a quick note asking my boss if I could go. He approved the seminar and paid for the entire trip.

The Dallas sunshine felt fantastic on my pale Michigan skin. I was feeling very relieved and grateful for the break. I quickly checked into my hotel room and was headed out the door to the bar when my phone rang. I had a coworker travel to Dallas with me and he was asking if I was going to go to Zig Ziglar's house that night. I had completely forgotten the main speaker, Zig Ziglar, had invited everyone to his home the night before the seminar started. Dang it! I really wanted to get some drinks and sit in the sunshine. *Isn't it strange to go to the speaker's home? What could the purpose be?* Since work was paying for this trip, I did the responsible thing and caught the bus to his home.

I'm glad I went to his home instead of the hotel bar. I woke up refreshed and rested with the extra sleep. I signed in and quickly surveyed all the people there. I thought there would be more people attending the conference. The room was small and intimate. It was set up with round tables, a lot of flashing lights, and loud music. I felt completely out of place. I had never been to something this alive before. Everyone was nice, almost too nice, and that kind of irritated me. *What in the world was I doing here? What did Janet send me to?*

Oh well. I was already looking forward to the first break and some more sweet Dallas sunshine. In an effort to hide a little, I took a seat towards the back and watched as a group of people surrounded Zig Ziglar. He was smiling and shaking hands with everyone. I was studying him to see what type of person he was. People were hugging him. *Who hugs people at a conference? Weird.* As I watched, it did seem as though he genuinely cared. He seemed to be engaging each person and not just going through the motions. I made a mental note to watch closely to see if I could catch him being real. Then, the music stopped and the first speaker introduced Zig Ziglar. *Where in the world am I? Why are these people so happy?*

Over the course of the next three days, I met some amazing people who shared their stories and filled me in on just exactly who Zig Ziglar was and, more importantly, how his books and tapes had changed their lives. My head was spinning because I couldn't fathom a book or a person changing your life. *Is this a cult or something?*

Zig spent a significant amount of time teaching about PMA, or, positive mental attitude. He said, "People often say that motivation doesn't last. Well, neither does bathing - that's why we recommend it daily."

Zig was funny, entertaining and engaging. He made me laugh and I love to laugh. He was nothing like anyone I had ever worked with. The main theme of the conference was "You can get everything in life you want if you will just help enough other people get what they want." The more I watched our featured speaker, the more I could see he actually lived the theme he was teaching.

Digesting all the positivity sounded great at the conference, but relating it to work and my life seemed impossible. I was very critical because clearly he didn't know the negative environment I worked in and all the problems I faced on a regular basis. I sat back with my arms crossed and a scowl on my face.

They handed out a sheet was titled the DiSC, A Personal Profile Assessment. At this time, we were supposed to answer questions and fill in the chart which correlated to our answers. I answered the questions as though I was at work. I charted my answers and waited for them to go over the results. The results were revealing and I didn't like what I heard about myself. This was when everything on the inside of me started to crumble just a little.

And I don't crumble.

Ever.

I am the fourth of five kids.

I grew up on a dirt road in Michigan.

My parents loved us and worked extremely hard to put us through college.

I earned a varsity letter in three different sports in high school.

I graduated in the Top Ten of my high school.

I earned my Bachelor of Science in Manufacturing Systems Engineering from GMI Engineering & Management Institute (now Kettering University) in Flint, Michigan.

My parents taught me to work hard and love my family. I value toughness. I am very competitive. I win or I don't play. I like control. I had a plan for my future and nothing was going to stop me.

> *I had a plan for my future and nothing was going to stop me.*

As I looked over the results, my stomach felt sick. I didn't know what to do with this *crumbling. Can you imagine seeing yourself in the mirror for the first time?* I was twenty-six years old and had no clue. To really see yourself as others see you is debilitating when it doesn't line up with how you see yourself. I merely thought I was a hard worker. *Isn't that all that counts?* The DiSC did described some positives about my personality. Big Deal.

All I could focus on was: "overuses control of people and situations to accomplish his/her own results" and "being so focused on results, they often may lack empathy and seem uncaring" and "developers are capable of manipulating people and situations". One really hard hitting description read "developers are apt to become belligerent" because I had been labeled this as a kid. Insides CRUMBLING.

My mind was spinning and I was starting to understand why I would get angry or frustrated at work. I felt uneasy heading into the next exercise. Zig Ziglar designed *The Wheel of Life*[2] as a way of showing us how we need to distribute our time, our focus, and where we need to set goals. Most of us can focus heavily in one or a few areas...The issue is we leave the others unattended.

Picture in your mind the words: CAREER, PERSONAL, PHYSICAL, FAMILY, MENTAL, FINANCIAL, and SPIRITUAL. All of the words are placed at the ends of the spokes on a wheel. At the center of the wheel was the number zero and at the end of each spoke was the number ten. Having all tens meant the perfect wheel was created. The trainer asked us to take a moment and rank these areas of our life with a number and then connect the dots to see what our wheel looked like.

I ranked CAREER at a seven, PERSONAL at a seven, PHYSICAL at a six, FAMILY at a seven, MENTAL at a seven, FINANCIAL at a seven, SPIRITUAL at a (generous) two. I did as I was instructed and connected my dots revealing my personal Wheel of Life.

[2] https://www.ziglar.com/articles/the-wheel-of-life/

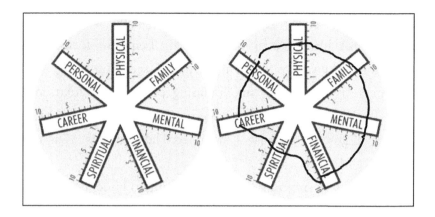

Zig stepped onto the stage and started to train. He really knew how to light up a room with his smile and wisdom. He took the Wheel of Life and made it personal. One particular question changed everything for me, "Let's say this was the tire on your bicycle that you ride in your life, how is your ride? Bumpy? Smooth? Everything good for a while and then flat?"

Oh. I quickly lost my breath. It was as if I had been punched in the stomach. I couldn't breathe because he perfectly described my life. Everything would go well and then flat – for periods of time. *Why? What area was causing the flat part and making my life bumpy?* I looked closer at the chart and it was flat on the spiritual spoke.

For the rest of the seminar Zig Ziglar, one of the best motivators in the world, outlined some personal instruction for everyone in each of the different areas. Each person's wheel was different which meant the needs of those in the crowd were different. Yet, for the first time in my life, I was infused with hope for creating a better work-life and relationships. What he said made sense and deep inside I wanted to be more like him, he was absolutely mesmerizing and I found myself following him around just to get more time with him.

On the very last day of the conference, there was a birthday celebration titled *Born to Win*. Surprise! They even had cake and ice cream to celebrate. People were high fiving, hugging each other, and shaking hands. There were tears of happiness... And it wasn't weird at all. We were excited to go home and work on the new skills we had learned. It was a true celebration. I could feel the joy in the room.

I thought the conference was over and then the lead trainer made a special announcement telling us, off to her right, Zig would be sharing his personal testimony. We were welcome to join him or head over for cake. I didn't know what a testimony was, however I did know I was focused on learning as much as I could from Zig before I headed back to Michigan and my real life. My mind was changing for the better and it was exciting.

I found my way to the back row of the red cushioned chairs. I could smell the birthday cake and hear the buzz of everyone celebrating. If Zig had more to say, I had more to learn. So, off to the side, with no lights, music, or microphone, Zig began to share his personal testimony of when he met Jesus Christ.

He walked us through the first forty-five years of his life without Christ. He shared his personal conversion and life after he knew Christ. He talked about his daughter, Suzan, who had died of pulmonary fibrosis, a lung disease, and how he was absolutely sure he would see her again because of their shared faith in Jesus Christ.

At this point, Zig paused, looked right at us...right at me...and asked, "The question is, do you know the Lord? It's a given that all of us are going to die. I believe with all of my heart that heaven is a real place, that hell is a real place. We will go, by our choice to one of them. And I say by our choice because, you see, God's voted for you, Satan's voted against you. And the deciding vote is going to be yours."

I had never heard it put that way, before. It wasn't complicated. It wasn't some sort of system or a set of steps to get to God. Heaven and Hell was already decided and I just had to choose.

Every wall of toughness and control I had built up came crumbling down. My eyes began to swell with tears and my coworker handed me a cake napkin to wipe them away. My answer was simple and I knew my next steps. I didn't know the Lord and I knew, based on the last three days, I wanted to.

During Zig's testimony, he mentioned the book, *Confessions of a Happy Christian*, he wrote for his daughter while she was far from Jesus. I went directly to the table where they were selling books and bought it. Sadly, at twenty-six years of age, I had never finished a book. I read to get by in school and college because reading just wasn't my thing. I read this book cover to cover on the plane ride back to snowy Michigan.

The car ride home was the first indicator that life was about to get really different. I told Blake a little about the conference, but not everything, not the most important thing. Once I stopped talking, I leaned over to turn the music up and I was mortified at the song. I immediately asked Blake, in a not so nice tone, "WHAT IS THIS SONG?"

Blake replied with a completely puzzled look, "The same song you were listening to before you left for Dallas." I turned it off. I wasn't sure what to listen to but I sure knew I was not going to listen to that music again.

As life got back to normal, I definitely wasn't the same person. *Choosing Jesus changed me.*

I started reading more. I questioned my choices. Drinking, swearing, telling crude jokes at work, gossiping, judging coworkers, and watching certain television shows all came to a halt. I saw all of my actions differently because they mattered to someone other than me. I believed everything I did mattered to Jesus.

A few months later, Blake and I attended a wedding where I ran into my sorority sister, Susan. I asked her where she was working and she said that she found a job in the Grand Rapids area. After talking for a while, we figured out she lived right around the corner from us. I graduated 2 years before Susan and she knew I lived in a city north of Grand Rapids. My feelings were hurt because she hadn't called me, but then I remembered the *old Denise* Susan knew. I didn't blame her for not calling. Susan is a very sweet girl from the south. *Completely opposite of the old me.*

I remember washing dishes at the corner sink in my kitchen when the phone rang. Can you imagine my shock when it was Susan? She sounded nervous. She was calling to invite me to bible study. My life was about to drastically change… for the better.

As I sit in my family room on my old blue leather couch leading a neighborhood bible study, I'm still so grateful God used Janet and Susan to help connect me to Him. I'm scared to think what choices would have ruined my life if they would have ignored

Jesus' voice. What if Janet keeps the good she experienced at *Born to Win* to herself? What if Susan never calls and invites me to bible study?

Yes, it truly was a miracle to go to Dallas and hear one of the best motivational speakers of my time.

It was a miracle to choose Jesus.

It was a miracle when Jesus changed my heart and mind.

It was a miracle to be invited to bible study.

The effect of these miracles lives on to this very day. Susan's invite to bible study ignited a fire in my mind and soul that is still lit today. Susan also introduced me to the joy of being with other women who love Jesus. In the fall of 1998, I never knew how much I'd need Jesus in my life. With each women's bible study I have attended, I've met women I've desperately needed for my walk.

I can't believe it has been nineteen years since my *Born to Win* conference. I've been blessed to participate in many bible studies with Jesus loving women in 4 different cities. Early in my walk with Jesus, I was introduced to Beth Moore's bible studies. I will forever remember her teaching on Isaiah 43:2 (NIV) *"When you pass through the waters, I will be with you; and when you pass through the rivers they will not sweep over you. When you walk through the fire, you will not be burned; the flames will not set you ablaze."* She repeated over and over, "It is not IF the storm comes, it is WHEN." I was early in my walk with Jesus and I knew I was not ready for a storm.

Storms are different for all of us. Sometimes, it's the rain of a long day caring for children, other times, it's the torrential soaking of an overwhelming career or marriage, and still other times, the hurricanes of hopelessness arrive on our doorsteps. And, when the storms of life have blown against me, Jesus and women have held me together against the storms that have tried to destroy my life.

God has been beyond faithful as I have learned to give him control over my life. For me, this only comes through studying His word.

I've needed Him through three years of infertility.

I've needed Him through quitting my career and finding my identity in Him.

I've needed Him through five moves.

I've needed Him through two job losses.

I've needed Him through four Caesarian-Sections in five years.

I've needed Him through a miscarriage.

I've needed Him through my sister, Sharron's, cancer and death.

I've needed Him through my sister-in-law, Cathy's, cancer and death.

I've needed Him through twenty-two years of marriage.

At bible study tonight, one of the actions from *Favor with Kings* was to write down the dream you have for your life but are afraid to talk about out loud. I opened up and said that I had written down in my journal I wanted to write, speak, or work in women's ministry.

What a miracle (again) when, one month later, I was asked to write a chapter in this book of miracles...and it came together in my imperfect living room on a dust-covered coffee table.

Micah 7:15 (NIV):

"As in the days when you came out from the land of Egypt, I will show you miracles."

The Greatest Miracle

Each woman in this book is a recipient of the greatest miracle available to humankind: the gift of salvation. We have been saved by grace, through faith, (Ephesians 2:8) because of what Jesus did for us on the cross. Have you received the miraculous gift of salvation from Christ? Can you say you know you belong to Him and He belongs to you? If not, I invite you to pray this prayer and accept this incredible gift:

Father, I believe that your Son, Jesus, lived on this earth to ultimately die for me. I know I've sinned; I've missed the mark many times and I cannot save myself. I know that no amount of good deeds can wash me clean – but You can! Today, I choose to place my trust in the price you paid on the cross. I now turn from my sin and my own ways and I turn toward You. Your death and resurrection were enough to set me free! Thank You for dying for me, being my Savior, and giving me the gift of eternal life. Now, I ask your Holy Spirit to fill me with boldness and to guide me to live for You.

Amen.

The Miracle Effect was a miracle project; right down to the women God chose to participate in it. I am so grateful for each one of them! I would like to extend my heartfelt thanks to each co-author, who willingly put her soul on her sleeve, telling of the trials and tribulations that caused her to need a miracle in the first place, and the glory that ensued.

A special thank you to Reji Laberje, of Bucket List to Bookshelf, for helping to make the writing, editing, and marketing of this book an unforgettable experience for us all. Your tender-loving-care and expertise, as well as that of your fellow writing industry professional, Marla McKenna, were exactly what were needed to coax our stories out and give us the tools we needed to tell them to the world.

Thank you, Nada Orlic, for the breathtaking book cover, and Kimberly Laberge for the beautiful photos and video footage to accompany our miracle stories.

Most of all, I want to thank our Lord and Savior, Jesus Christ, the God of the Bible, for being true to His Word and showing us miracles.

Kimberly Joy Krueger
Founder
The Fellowship of Extraordinary Women
FEW International Publications

Made in the USA
Columbia, SC
20 March 2019